Liberty and Freedom

Liberty and Freedom

NORTH CAROLINA'S TOUR OF THE BILL OF RIGHTS

Edited by Kenrick N. Simpson

Office of Archives and History
North Carolina Department of Cultural Resources
Raleigh
2009

Printed by Edwards Brothers

CONTENTS

ILLUSTRATIONS

PREFACE

North Carolina's copy of the Bill of Rights has experienced a long and colorful history. Acting on behalf of Congress, President George Washington first sent the document to Gov. Samuel Johnston on October 2, 1789. Many opponents of ratification of the United States Constitution had insisted on a Bill of Rights to limit the federal government's power. A Bill of Rights also was seen as an inducement for North Carolina to join the Union. In 1788 North Carolina had refused to ratify the United States Constitution because it lacked a Bill of Rights. Washington's letter and the proposed Bill of Rights satisfied the state's concerns. North Carolina ratified both the Constitution and then the Bill of Rights in late 1789. Thereafter the Bill of Rights remained in the state's custody until the closing days of the Civil War. When Union troops occupied the State Capitol beginning on April 13, 1865, pillaging broke out. Numerous documents were removed, including the Bill of Rights. A Union soldier took North Carolina's copy of the Bill of Rights home to Ohio, where in 1866 he sold it for $5.00 to a fellow Ohioan who later became a businessman in Indiana. The document remained in the possession of that businessman's family for nearly 135 years. Publication of this volume in part explains how the document was recovered in March 2003 and returned to the citizens of North Carolina in August 2005.

To celebrate the return of the Bill of Rights, the Office of Archives and History in the North Carolina Department of Cultural Resources decided to bring the document to the people. During 2007 the document and accompanying exhibit, titled *Liberty and Freedom: North Carolina's Tour of the Bill of Rights*, traveled across the state. The North Carolina Museum of History built the exhibit, and the North Carolina State Archives secured, transported, and interpreted the document at each site. For 2007 the Department of Cultural Resources adopted as its theme, "History Happens Here." The exhibition of the Bill of Rights in seven Tar Heel cities expressed that theme perfectly. More than twenty thousand people visited the exhibit.

To expand further upon the interpretation of the Bill of Rights and its meaning to modern Americans, each of the selected sites hosted a keynote lecture. Each lecture focused on one or more of the rights protected by the Bill of Rights. Those lectures, ranging from freedom of the press to the right to a jury trial and due process, featured distinguished speakers in history and law. All but two of those lectures are published in this volume. The late Don Higginbotham, the Dowd Distinguished Professor of History emeritus at the University of North Carolina at Chapel Hill, spoke from notes on the Second Amendment, a topic on which he had lectured and published numerous times. Similarly, Walter Dellinger, the Douglas B. Maggs Professor of Law at the Duke University School of Law, presented his thoughts on non-enumerated rights in the Bill of Rights as a lecture without a written paper.

When the exhibit visited the North Carolina Museum of History in Raleigh during Constitution Week, September 17-23, 2007, a one-day symposium on the Bill of Rights included three additional speakers besides Walter Dellinger. Charlene Bickford, editor of the papers of the First Federal Congress at George Washington University, discussed the origins of the Bill of Rights and her role in authenticating and identifying North Carolina's copy. In addition, Dale Talbert and Karen Blum of the North Carolina Attorney General's Office discussed their role in establishing North Carolina's ownership of the document in both federal and state courts. Both of those lectures are included in this volume.

On March 24, 2008, the Wake County Superior Court ruled that North Carolina's copy of the Bill of Rights belonged to the state and hence the people of North Carolina. After five long years of litigation, North Carolinians could rejoice in the recovery of a document as important today as it was on the day of final ratification, December 15, 1791. The lectures collected in this volume offer a broad view of the many rights enjoyed by citizens of the United States. They provide historical perspective as well as legal insight into this uniquely American document. In the words of United States Supreme Court justice William J. Brennan, "The Framers of the Bill of Rights did not purport to 'create' rights. Rather, they designed the Bill of Rights to prohibit our Government from infringing rights and liberties presumed to be preexisting." In his first Inaugural Address, President Thomas Jefferson labeled the principles protected by the Constitution and the Bill of Rights as "the creed of our political faith—the text of civil instruction—the touchstone by which to try the services of those we trust; and should we wander from them in moments of error or alarm, let us hasten to retrace our steps and to regain the road which alone leads to peace, liberty, and safety." The Bill of Rights, written in the eighteenth century, remains a vital part of our political discourse in the twenty-first century.

Jeffrey J. Crow
Deputy Secretary
N.C. Office of Archives
and History

ACKNOWLEDGMENTS

Alan Westmoreland of the Archives and Records Section of the Office of Archives and History supplied the images in this volume from the Bill of Rights tour of the state. Shortly before his death, Alexander M. Rivera Jr. of Durham graciously consented to the use of his photograph of African Americans voting in South Carolina in 1948. In the Historical Publications Section, Kenrick N. Simpson edited the lectures for publication and prepared the index, Susan M. Trimble typeset the volume and created the cover, Lisa D. Bailey proofread the manuscript, and Donna E. Kelly, section administrator, ushered the volume through the publication process.

LIBERTY AND FREEDOM: NORTH CAROLINA'S TOUR OF THE BILL OF RIGHTS
2007

Tour Itinerary

Dates	Venues	Speakers
February 9-11	Airborne and Special Operations Museum, Fayetteville	William S. Price Jr.
March 9-11	Louise Wells Cameron Art Museum, Wilmington	Alan D. Watson
April 19-21	1767 Chowan County Courthouse, Edenton	Freddie L. Parker
September 17-23	North Carolina Museum of History, Raleigh	Charlene Bangs Bickford Karen Blum and W. Dale Talbert Walter Dellinger
October 5-7	ImaginOn Center, Charlotte	Julius L. Chambers
November 8-10	University of North Carolina at Asheville	Willis P. Whichard
November 30-December 2	Greensboro Historical Museum, Greensboro	Don Higginbotham

The 1767 Chowan County Courthouse was the third stop on the *Liberty and Freedom* traveling exhibit tour. In addition to the Bill of Rights in its special display case, designed and built by craftsmen at the North Carolina Museum of History, the exhibit included several standing panels that illustrated the genesis of the document, its mysterious history after disappearing from the State Capitol in 1865, and its recovery in 2003. Image courtesy of the State Archives, N.C. Office of Archives and History, Raleigh.

Text of the Proposed Bill of Rights

Congress of the United States begun and held at the City of New York, on Wednesday the fourth of March, one thousand seven hundred and eighty nine.

THE Conventions of a number of the States, having at the time of their adopting the Constitution, expressed a desire, in order to prevent misconstruction or abuse of its powers, that further declaratory and restrictive clauses should be added: And as extending the ground of public confidence in the Government will best ensure the beneficent ends of its institution.

RESOLVED by the Senate and House of Representatives of the United States of America in Congress assembled, two thirds of both Houses concurring, that the following Articles be proposed to the Legislatures of the several States, as amendments to the Constitution of the United States all, or any of which Articles, when ratified by three fourths of the said Legislatures, to be valid to all intents and purposes as part of the said Constitution; vizt.

ARTICLES in addition to and amendment of the Constitution of the United States of America, proposed by Congress, and ratified by the Legislatures of the several States, pursuant to the fifth Article of the original Constitution.

Article the First. After the first enumeration required by the first article of the Constitution, there shall be one Representative for every thirty thousand, until the number shall amount to one hundred, after which the proportion shall be so regulated by Congress, that there shall be not less than one hundred Representatives, nor less than one Representative for every forty thousand persons, until the number of Representatives shall amount to two hundred, after which the proportion shall be so regulated by Congress, that there shall not be less than two hundred Representatives, nor more than one Representative for every fifty thousand persons.

Article the Second. No law varying the compensation for the services of the Senators and Representatives, shall take effect, until an election of Representatives shall have intervened.

Article the Third. Congress shall make no law respecting an establishment of religion, or prohibiting the free exercise thereof; or abridging the freedom of speech, or of the press; or the right of the people peaceably to assemble and to petition the Government for a redress of grievances.

Article the Fourth. A well regulated Militia, being necessary to the security of a free State, the right of the people to keep and bear Arms, shall not be infringed.

Article the Fifth. No Soldier shall in time of peace be quartered in any house, without the consent of the Owner, nor in time of war, but in a manner to be prescribed by law.

Article the Sixth. The right of the people to be secure in their persons, houses, papers, and effects, against unreasonable searches and seizures, shall not be violated, and no Warrants shall issue, but upon probable cause supported by oath or affirmation, and particularly describing the place to be searched, and the persons or things to be seized.

Article the Seventh. No person shall be held to answer for a capital or otherwise infamous crime, unless on a presentment or indictment of a Grand Jury, except in cases arising in the land or naval forces, or in the militia when in actual service in time of War or public danger; nor shall any person be subject for the same offence to be twice put in jeopardy of life or limb; nor shall be compelled in any criminal case to be a witness against himself, nor be deprived of life, liberty or property, without due process of law, nor shall private property be taken for public use, without just compensation.

Article the Eighth. In all criminal prosecutions, the accused shall enjoy the right to a speedy and public trial, by an impartial jury of the State and district where the crime shall have been committed, which district shall have been previously ascertained by law, and to be informed of the nature and cause of the accusation; to be confronted with the witnesses against him, to have compulsory process for obtaining witnesses in his favor, and to have the assistance of Counsel for his defence.

Article the Ninth. In Suits at common law, where the value in controversy shall exceed twenty dollars, the right of trial by Jury shall be preserved, and no fact tried by a Jury shall be otherwise re examined in any Court of the United States than according to the rules of the common law.

Article the Tenth. Excessive bail shall not be required, nor excessive fines imposed, nor cruel and unusual punishments inflicted.

Article the Eleventh. The enumeration in the Constitution of certain rights, shall not be Construed to deny or disparage others retained by the people.

Article the Twelfth. The powers not delegated to the United States by the Constitution, nor prohibited by it to the States, are reserved to the States respectively, or to the people.

Frederick Augustus Muhlenberg Speaker of the House of Representatives
John Adams, Vice President of the United States and President of the Senate
Attest.
John Beckley Clerk of the House of Representatives
Sam A. Otis Secretary of the Senate

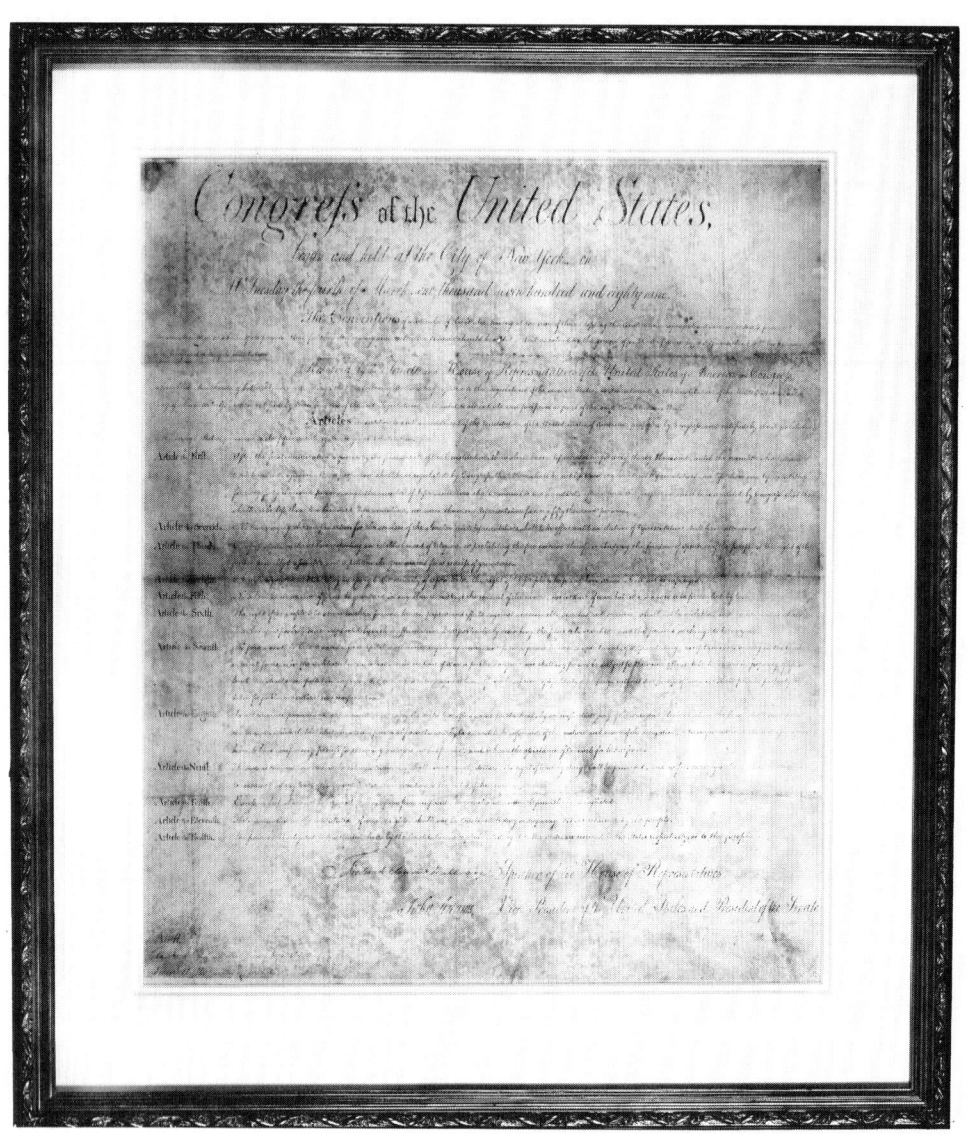

North Carolina's original copy of the Bill of Rights. Image courtesy of the State Archives, N.C. Office of Archives and History, Raleigh.

SACRED LIBERTY: FREEDOM OF THE PRESS IN AMERICA

By William S. Price Jr.

EDITOR'S NOTE: Over the course of a long and distinguished career in the field of public history, Dr. William S. Price Jr. has served the North Carolina historical community as editor, administrator, author, and teacher. A native North Carolinian, he graduated from Duke University in 1963 with a bachelor's degree in history. After serving as an officer in the U.S. Navy, including a tour of duty in Vietnam in 1966, Price returned to school and earned a masters degree (1969) and a doctorate (1973) from the University of North Carolina at Chapel Hill. He began his first career in public history with the then Department of Archives and History in 1971 as head of the Colonial Records Project in the Historical Publications Section. In 1975 he was promoted to assistant director of the Division of Archives and History, and from 1981 to 1995 he served as director of the division. After retirement from state service, Dr. Price occupied the chair of the Kenan Professor of History at Meredith College in Raleigh, where he was instrumental in developing a major in public history. He retired from Meredith in 2006. He is currently the North Caroliniana Scholar in Residence at Peace College. During his stint with the Colonial Records Project, he edited *North Carolina Higher-Court Records, 1702-1708* (volume IV of the Second Series of *Colonial Records*), which received an Award of Merit from the American Association for State and Local History in 1975, and *North Carolina Higher-Court Minutes, 1709-1723* (volume V). Dr. Price also served as a consultant in the publication of *The Way We Lived in North Carolina*, which received the James Harvey Robinson Prize from the American Historical Association in 1984. He is the author of a book, *"There Ought to Be a Bill of Rights": North Carolina Enters a New Nation* (1991), and most recently, *Nathaniel Macon of North Carolina: Three Views of His Character and Creed* (2008). He delivered these remarks during the first stop on the Bill of Rights tour, at the Airborne and Special Operations Museum in Fayetteville on February 9, 2007.

In October 1789, President George Washington forwarded twelve just-proposed amendments to the new Constitution to the eleven states then in the Union and to North Carolina and Rhode Island, which he hoped would soon join. The first two of those amendments were structural proposals relating to the proportion of congressional representation and rules regulating salary increases. Neither of them would be ratified in 1791 when the other ten were. First among those ten was a statement of major civil liberties that most American political leaders saw as fundamental rights: free exercise of religion without any established church, the right of peaceful assembly and petition to correct grievances, and freedom of speech and of the press. If it seems odd that so many basic rights were grouped together in what became the First Amendment, that concern is dispelled when we consider that the original purpose of the Bill of Rights was to limit the powers of the national, federal government. For instance, the federal government could not prohibit free exercise of religion, but a state might well choose to do so. The North Carolina Constitution of 1776, despite its guarantee that "all men have a right to worship Almighty God according to the dictates of their own conscience," prohibited those "who shall deny the being of God, or the truth of the Protestant religion, or the authority of either the Old or

New Testaments" from holding any office in state government. Many other states had similar restrictions and deliberately so.

It is important to remember that prior to ratification of the Thirteenth Amendment to the U.S. Constitution in 1865, the Bill of Rights circumscribed the national government far more than those of the states. After all, virtually every state had its own bill of rights or other legislative or judicial protections of civil liberties. If the Constitution of 1787 was a triumph of the Federalists, the Bill of Rights four years later was the high-water mark of the Anti-Federalists. Their insistence on written guarantees of individual freedoms and clear curbs on national authority led James Madison and others to abandon their earlier opposition to a bill of rights.

A major historian of the early nation, Robert A. Rutland, has noted that "the Salem witchcraft trials [1692] and the adoption of the Federal Bill of Rights virtually opened and closed the eighteenth century; and that those historical incidents indicate the tremendous intellectual advancement during that stirring span of time." That George Washington, John Adams, and Thomas Jefferson flourished in the same time frame is quite remarkable. Had our revolution occurred in, say, 1726 or 1826 rather than 1776, our constitution would be a far less durable instrument than it has proven to be. One has only to read Carl Becker's classic work on the Declaration of Independence to realize how fortunate we are that our founding documents were written and adopted at the apex of the Age of Enlightenment. There was a profounder regard for the potential of human reason at that time than in any era before or since.

Over the last few decades, historians have rightly been more attentive to the diversity and complexity of social and cultural influences on the development of our nation. To acknowledge the importance of ordinary men and women and multiple ethnicities in early America is not to diminish this fundamental reality: the America that declared its independence from Great Britain was English in institutions as basic as its principal language and its concept of law.

As early as 1578, when Queen Elizabeth issued a charter to Sir Humphrey Gilbert, half brother of Walter Raleigh, for settling colonists in America, she had said: "[Settlers] being either born within our said Realms of England or Ireland, or in any other place within our allegiance . . . shall and may have and enjoy all the privileges of free denizens and persons native of England . . . as if they were born and personally resident within our said Realm of England." The same or similar wording appeared in the 1584 charter to Raleigh that led to the Roanoke settlements and in the Virginia Charter of 1606, as well as in most subsequent Crown charters to colonies in British North America. This royal grant of the rights of Englishmen to American settlers was hugely significant, and it differed sharply from the practices of other colonial powers, such as Spain and Portugal. The British Crown thus imparted to its colonists a deep appreciation for and identification with the English tradition of individual freedoms. Every freeholder, whether in England or Virginia, was entitled to protection of life, liberty, and property from arbitrary government. Nor were such ideals of freedom new, for the foremost safeguards in English law—the writ of habeas corpus and trial by jury—predated Magna Carta of 1215.

English Puritans' opposition to executive tyranny in the 1640s deeply affected settlers migrating to America in the second half of the seventeenth century. The Glorious Revolution of 1689 offered additional inspiration to colonists who valued their civil liberties. Feudalism, with its well-defined class structure topped by an aristocracy of inherited titles, did not cross the Atlantic, and this circumstance made Americans even more likely to claim certain rights than were Englishmen. By the 1760s, Americans were practicing a government more firmly rooted in notions of civil rights than were their counterparts in the mother country. One has only to scan the explosion of pamphlets generated in opposition to the Stamp Act in 1765 to gain a sense that Americans saw themselves as heirs to and defenders of traditional British rights against arbitrary and tyrannical government.

The fairly wide availability of printing presses in America had made the large distribution of Stamp Act tracts possible. The seventeenth century had seen a steady expansion in the number of printers in England and America publishing pamphlets, newspapers, broadsides, and books. Almost from the introduction of printing in England in the fifteenth century, publishing had been viewed as "a matter of state," and printers were required to obtain a government license in order to practice their craft. There were few problems with this system early on. However, with the outpouring of literature as brief as a broadside or as long as a book during the Puritan revolt in the 1640s, Parliament sought to rein in aspects of this production that threatened civil order. In 1643, the House of Lords and the House of Commons ordered the destruction of unlicensed presses and the confiscation of illegal literature. The following year, England's greatest living writer, John Milton, wrote *Areopagitica* to promote liberty for unlicensed printing. Milton's basic argument is that truth will prevail in a contest of ideas. God has invested us with free will, and we alone must exercise it, not some outside agency. Even bad ideas have their good uses. As Milton says, "bad books . . . to a discreet and judicious reader serve in many respects to discover, to confute, to forewarn, and to illustrate." Freedom strengthens the loyalty of a citizenry; suppression undermines it. Although of little immediate impact, Milton's work would subsequently become a touchstone of freedom of the press arguments from the eighteenth century until today.

Responding to the growth and popularity of newspapers in 1694, Parliament freed the press from "prior restraint" in publishing except when reporting on Parliament's own proceedings. In the middle of the eighteenth century, the great legal scholar William Blackstone clarified the meaning of that action and the body of common law preceding it: "The liberty of the press consists in laying no *previous* restraints upon publications." But if a publication libeled, blasphemed, or promoted immorality or sedition, it was subject to legal action. As Blackstone put it, "Every freeman has the undoubted right to lay what sentiments he pleases before the public: to forbid this is to destroy freedom of the press: but if he publishes what is improper, mischievous, or illegal, he must take the consequences." The subsequent history of freedom of the press in America was and still is measured against the question of whether a publication unwarrantedly damages either an individual or the common good.

Setting aside consideration of personal libels and matters of creative expression that some might define as obscene, freedom of the press in its most public form relates to its watchdog role in the operations of government and other large institutions. From about 1700 on, whether in Britain or North America, the government officials' greatest concern about the press was its potential for encouraging sedition, disturbing the public peace, and generating resistance and rebellion. The eminent historian Leonard Levy has argued at length that the eighteenth-century American's concept of freedom of the press followed Blackstone's views. He demonstrates that in the swirl of debates in both infant state and national forums in the 1770s and 1780s whenever a free press was mentioned, it was in line with the British model of no prior restraint but potential action for illegal statements once in print. Levy points out that the only constitutional framer to speak about his understanding of a free press was Hugh Williamson of North Carolina. In 1788, he commended the British model. Not even so profound a thinker as Thomas Jefferson had much to say on the matter prior to the 1790s. While he did endorse prosecutions for seditious libel in the 1780s, Jefferson opposed any legal action against publication of accurate information. His reservation hearkens back to the most famous early test of a free press in pre-Revolutionary America—the *Zenger* case.

In the fall of 1733, John Peter Zenger operated a newspaper in New York that frequently attacked royal governor William Cosby. After a year of this, Zenger was arrested for libel and jailed for ten months before trial. When the case proceeded in the summer of 1735, Zenger's attorney, Andrew Hamilton, defied admonitions from the bench and argued that the jury was fully capable of determining the truth of his client's statements. The jury acquitted Zenger, who soon published an account of his trial that circulated widely in Britain and its colonies. There were a few other cases in England and America during the 1700s in which truth would serve as a successful defense in libel actions, but none of them supplanted Blackstone's mid-century definition. Zenger's triumph in 1735, like Milton's *Areopagitica* in 1644, was more important as historical precedent in later years than it was among its contemporaries. Prior to the transforming ideology of the American Revolution, free speech (a close cousin to a free press) was chiefly a parliamentary privilege rather than a civil right, and written or spoken criticism of government (colonial assemblies as well as Parliament) was vigorously suppressed. Still, the colonial press was a bit freer in America than its counterpart in Britain—in part because an ocean separated it from London and made the Crown and its government seem less awesome.

As the revolution drew nearer, more and more Americans began to concern themselves with defining their civil rights in writing. In the fall of 1774, the First Continental Congress adopted a Declaration of Rights enumerating various basic freedoms like jury trial and petition and assembly. The last liberty listed was that of the press, "without which a people cannot be free and happy." The Congress concluded that the press must be free in "its ready communication of thoughts between subjects, and its consequential promotion of union among them." The Stamp Act crisis a decade earlier and subsequent measures like the Townsend Acts had shown Americans the importance of the press in spreading information to an anxious public from New England to the South and of helping to define a sense of common cause and purpose. With this congressional action, a group of public officials had for the first time declared freedom of the press an essential liberty. In the subsequent constitution making that would occur in the former colonies after combat commenced in 1775, nine of the eleven new state constitutions guaranteed a free press in one way or another. The Virginia Declaration of Rights in June 1776 called freedom of the press "one of the great bulwarks of liberty," and Virginia sent copies of this document to every colony, where whole sections of it would appear in the bills of rights of seven states from Vermont to North Carolina.

Yet by 1778, every state had passed laws restricting spoken or written statements that were contrary to the revolutionary cause or critical of Congress, state government, or public officials. What was going on here? Was the press free or not? Were the founders hypocrites or heroes? In seeking an answer, it is essential to remember that the dividing line between civil liberties and public safety in times of crisis (as the 1770s certainly were) can be fragile. The founders who proclaimed freedom of the press in 1776 and then voted to suppress it two years later saw no hypocrisy in their actions. For them, the ideal of liberty remained vital, but the close proximity of wartime dangers necessitated certain measures of control. One has only to think of our current struggles over our idealistic revolutionary legacy in the tense times since September 11, 2001, to grasp some of the dilemmas confronting lawmakers in the 1770s.

As Americans sought to define their nationhood in the 1780s, the effort to fix a workable national government unfolded. The obstacles to achieving a viable central government in the Articles of Confederation of 1781 seemed obvious to many, and by 1787 a new constitution was submitted to the states for approval. The chief architect of the document, James Madison, and others who supported a stronger national government resisted the call of their opponents (soon deemed Anti-Federalists) for provisions guarding individuals' and states' rights. Federalist proponents countered that any enumeration of such rights could raise the awful prospect of some future tyrant working to subvert them. As James Iredell stated at the first North Carolina ratification convention in Hillsborough in 1788, "A bill of rights, as I conceive, would not only be incongruous, but dangerous. No man, let his ingenuity be what it will, could enumerate all the individual rights not relinquished by this constitution." England had needed Magna Carta and the 1689 Bill of Rights precisely because it lacked what was now being offered in America: a *written* constitution that delineated and thus limited federal powers.

As ratification proceeded state by state starting with Delaware, the most frequently voiced objection was the absence of a bill of rights. When North Carolina declined to ratify at Hillsborough, it issued a clear call for further safeguards to be written into the Constitution. Indeed, when James Madison (who by 1788 had realized that a bill of rights must be added) introduced his dozen amendments in Congress the following summer, he said that he was doing so in part to encourage North Carolina to join the Union. North Carolina obliged in November 1789 in Fayetteville; the twelfth of the original thirteen to ratify, it was the third state to approve the ten amendments deemed the Bill of Rights.

Despite its endorsements in the First Continental Congress, through its inclusion in most state constitutions, to its elevated placement in the First

Amendment, the meaning of a free press was not entirely clear. If there was a more liberal view of the principle in America than existed in late-eighteenth-century England (and there surely was), it had nevertheless not achieved a uniformly accepted definition. Freedom of the press was nearly as amorphous in meaning as a term like "family values" is now. While there was a consensus in 1789 that the role of the press in disseminating information and ideas to the public was critically important in a nation where the citizens, not a monarch, were sovereign, there was still a wariness of its potential for promoting sedition, especially in unsettled times. Within a decade, though, a new national crisis would help to shape our understanding of a free press as nothing else had done before.

By the time John Adams succeeded George Washington early in 1797, the Constitution was not yet ten years old. Among the things that had occurred during that time were some developments that troubled Washington and many others. Political partisanship had grown markedly, with Federalists like Alexander Hamilton and Adams on one side and Democratic-Republicans led by Jefferson and Madison on the other. Each side had its own allied newspapers, best exemplified by John Fenno's pro-Federalist *Gazette of the United States* and Philip Freneau's pro-Republican *National Gazette*. Both journals were based in Philadelphia where they engaged in vitriolic attacks on one another that resonated far beyond the City of Brotherly Love. Having a newspaper promoting a party's agenda became a key to political success in the 1790s, and this explains why North Carolina's leading Republican, Nathaniel Macon, urged Joseph Gales to abandon his journalism career in Philadelphia to move southward and start the *Raleigh Register* in 1799. That paper was crucial to Jefferson's triumph in the state the following year.

Another problem confronting Adams and the nation at the start of his presidency was the dismal situation in Europe. The French Revolution had veered away from the lofty sentiments and republican hopes of its start into open hostilities with other countries and the stark efficiency of the guillotine at home. Federalists tended to sympathize with Britain in these hard times; Republicans, remembering French support against British tyranny in our revolution and hoping that enlightened reason might yet prevail in France, favored the land of Lafayette. As British and French ships attacked one another on the high seas, American vessels bound for Caribbean and European ports found themselves subject to raids by both navies. By the time of Adams's inauguration, the French depredations were more severe, and formal diplomatic relations ceased.

As the situation deteriorated into undeclared war, divisions between Federalists and Republicans became even more pronounced and partisan newspaper attacks in nearly every state more venomous. In this poisoned atmosphere, Federalists proposed a series of bills in 1798 that Republicans saw as a blatant effort to silence their opposition. The four bills that President Adams signed into law were the Alien and Sedition Acts. Not only were they overtly political and clearly aimed at Republicans and their supporters, but the three acts pointed at aliens (especially French and Irish residents who generally favored Republicans) also never resulted in a single deportation. They were meant to intimidate and threaten more than anything else. The Sedition Act did those things and more. It criminalized any conspiracy against the government and forbade writing or speaking anything of a "false, scandalous, and malicious" nature against any government official. Furthermore, the act was to expire after the next election, thereby cynically demonstrating that its Federalist advocates recognized it for what it was—a short-term measure to silence Republican critics. Of fourteen prosecutions under the law, all were directed at Republicans. The two leading Republican newspapers of New York City closed down under threat of prosecution. But as is often the case in overtly political lawmaking, the indictments backfired. Because of the prominence of many of the accused, some of the top legal minds in the nation rose to their defense and offered strong arguments in support of a free press.

Republicans in Congress and throughout the states had vigorously opposed the Alien and Sedition Acts. In the House of Representatives particularly, the debates were skillfully argued by Albert Gallatin of Pennsylvania, Edward Livingston of New York, and Nathaniel Macon of North Carolina. Indeed, it was Macon's prominence in the 1798 opposition that influenced Thomas Jefferson to support him as Speaker of the House in 1801. Not only did Macon argue that the legislation was clearly unconstitutional, but also that if Congress could abridge a free press, it could establish a national church as well since both were part of the First Amendment. "The liberty of the press is sacred, and ought to be left where the Constitution had left it," he said. Macon also observed that "The people suspect something is not right, when free discussion is feared by Government." With Gallatin and Livingston in the lead, Republicans abandoned any lingering notions of common law limitations on the press. They rejected the crime of seditious libel. A free government cannot be *criminally* attacked by the *opinions* of its citizens, or else it is not free. Overt acts or deeds might be injurious, but words cannot be. Free government depends on free exchange, and where the people are sovereign they must be informed by a competition of ideas. The press assists ordinary citizens in understanding the work of government more ably than the government itself can. An informed citizenry is the surest check on tyranny, and it alone should judge licentiousness through the jury process, when necessary. Echoing John Milton a century and a half earlier, Republicans argued that truth will triumph in the contest of ideas.

The Sedition Act did more to push Americans towards a libertarian view of a free press than anything else since the early days of the Revolution. After 1800, the burden fell increasingly on the federal government to prove that a publication was conspicuously harmful to the public good in order to warrant legal action against it. In the scales of justice, the balance tipped slightly but steadily in the press's favor from that point on.

It is instructive for Tar Heels who ponder Nathaniel Macon's activities in Congress in 1798 to also consider those of Edenton's James Iredell as a U.S. Supreme Court justice the following year. In hearing the case of John Fries of Pennsylvania for treason, Iredell had occasion to comment on the Sedition Act. Like John Marshall, he justified the law based on the "necessary and proper" clause of the Constitution. Iredell reasoned that since the framers surely knew Blackstone's definition of a free press, they must have accepted it. Punishment for libels under common law principles was necessary for a government to be able to protect itself from sedition. Within months of one another, two North Carolinians in national office thus came down on either side of the main

North Carolinians Nathaniel Macon (*left*) and James Iredell (*right*) adopted oppositional viewpoints regarding the freedom of the press under the Sedition Act of 1798. Images courtesy of the State Archives, N.C. Office of Archives and History, Raleigh.

arguments concerning freedom of the press—reflecting the division's not only in their home state but also in the whole nation. James Iredell would not live to see the Federalist position rejected in the elections of 1800, which put Thomas Jefferson in the White House and Republicans in control of Congress. As the premier historian of the Alien and Sedition Acts, James Morton Smith, has noted, "[The Sedition Act] resulted in the repudiation of the party which tried to protect itself behind [it]."

During the nineteenth century, notable presidents had their own problems with the press. For instance, Andrew Jackson opposed the postal service transmitting inflammatory antislavery literature in 1835, and Abraham Lincoln actually closed two newspapers in New York City that printed a bogus and highly incendiary draft proclamation in 1864. In the previous year, mob violence by draft resisters had wrought much destruction in Gotham, and the president clearly dreaded a repeat performance. Yet where the legislative branch was concerned, Congress did not limit speech and publications again until our entry into World War I, when it passed the so-called Sedition Act of 1918. It was repealed three years later. In 1940, the Alien Registration Act (known as the Smith Act) made any advocacy of violent overthrow of government a crime and was used against Communists and their supporters in the 1940s and 1950s.

It should be noted that individual state actions could and did continue to restrict the press, albeit often in indirect ways, even after the federal debacle of 1798-1800. For instance, in 1860 North Carolina convicted Daniel Worth, a Methodist minister, of distributing the antislavery book, *The Impending Crisis of the South* (by native Tar Heel Hinton Rowan Helper), in Guilford and Randolph counties. Worth was prosecuted and convicted under an 1830 law enacted in response to the earlier *Appeal to the Coloured Citizens of the World* (1829) by David Walker, a free black who had fled North Carolina for Boston. Walker's *Appeal* advocated the overthrow of slavery, by violence if necessary. While the state was unable to prosecute the out-of-state publisher of Helper's book, it could and did go after its in-state distributor.

With ratification of the Fourteenth Amendment in 1868, freedom of the press matters have moved increasingly out of state courts and into federal ones. Two of the most important Supreme Court decisions in the last half of the twentieth century have further defined freedom of the press. In *New York Times v. Sullivan* (1964), the Court invalidated a libel judgment won by an Alabama police commissioner. The commissioner had sued the *Times* for publishing a full-page paid advertisement containing some inaccuracies about his activities during the civil rights struggle; however, the *Times* did not print his name. The highest court held that public figures must establish "actual malice" in order to collect, and that a publisher must know the statements to be false or must demonstrate "a reckless disregard for the truth." In the famous Pentagon Papers case (*New York Times v. U.S.*) during the Vietnam War, the Supreme Court held in 1971 that the government had not shown that publication of the papers would do "identifiable harm" to specific individuals and therefore could proceed. Sometimes overlooked in that decision was the statement that once the documents were published, the government might still prosecute if materials libeled individuals or if reporters engaged in a crime to obtain documents.

More recently the federal courts have been called into the Valerie Plame matter in which Ms. Plame's identity as a CIA agent was compromised. Journalist Matt Cooper of *Time* magazine and Judith Miller of the *New York Times* sought protection from having to reveal their unnamed sources in reporting on the Plame affair in 2005, but the courts declined to oblige. While several states have shield laws to protect anonymous sources when revealing the truth, the federal government does not.

Freedom of speech and press were placed side by side in the Bill of Rights. Even before 1776, free speech and a free press have been more closely linked in America than in England. Both freedoms fall under the rubric of free expression, which British courts tend to define more narrowly than do ours. Our doctrine of popular sovereignty commits us to greater latitude for unpopular, provocative, and even offensive expression (with the possible exception of certain forms of sexual expression) than many other western cultures allow. "We the People" ultimately determine what the public good is. Yet if speech and press share classification as "expression," there remain fundamental differences that account for some of their distinctions. Publication lends a permanence that the spoken word does not. It can also provide an anonymity that speech cannot. Consider the extensive use of pseudonyms and aliases by eighteenth-century revolutionary writers. The great American diplomat George Kennan wrote as "X" after World War II to outline the strategy of containment that ultimately brought down the Soviet Union without a nuclear war. Even as twenty-first-century technologies blur some of the longtime definitions of publication, print still offers a means of documentation and permanence that computer screens cannot match. As any archivist will tell you, there are far more documents on paper since the advent of computers than there ever were before. How often do we print out words or images from our computer screens and then file them away using the same principles that would have guided a clerk of court in, say, seventeenth-century Chowan County?

Any current journalist will tell you that the press is changing rapidly and, in many cases, drastically. Consider the rise of blogs, for instance. Yet the role of a free press in informing and challenging its readers (or its viewers, if you prefer) is as important now as it ever was. Free governments chosen by their citizens must be accountable for their actions, and what better watchdog is there than a vigilant, even skeptical press? Twenty years from now, the transmission of "news" and ideas may be through means that we cannot currently envision. Information technology is changing at a staggering pace. But the technology is less valuable than the information it transmits. Our history shows us clearly that a free press is vital to a free society. Despite its occasional faults and imperfections, freedom of the press remains, as Nathaniel Macon characterized it in 1798, a sacred liberty.

SUGGESTED READINGS

With the advent and current widespread availability of the Internet, large numbers of people can access primary sources at various locations. Both the Library of Congress and the National Archives have superb collections available online in highly useable formats, as do various colleges and universities. The basic documents of American government dating from before the Declaration of Independence through the Bill of Rights and beyond are easily summoned to the computer screen. Well worth examining also are the debates over ratification of the Constitution in the various states as well as the journals of the Constitutional Convention of 1787 and of early meetings of the U.S. Congress. One cautionary note: When using search engines like the widely available Google or Yahoo, choose those sites that are demonstrably credible from the menu of choices that will be offered. That is, the Library of Congress, the National Archives, and various well-known universities will offer thoroughly reliable texts; some others may not.

There is an immense amount of secondary literature on the Bill of Rights from its antecedents to its most recent interpretation by courts. An excellent starting point for serious readers is Gaspare J. Saladino, "The Bill of Rights: A Bibliographic Essay," in *The Bill of Rights and the States: The Colonial and Revolutionary Origins of American Liberties*, edited by Patrick T. Conley and John P. Kaminski (Madison, Wis.: Madison House, 1992). That same book contains essays on the struggle over the Bill of Rights in the fourteen states where it was debated. My essay therein, " 'There Ought To Be a Bill of Rights': North Carolina Enters a New Nation," is also available as a book published by the Office of Archives and History in Raleigh. Most helpful as a broad overview of the legal history of the document is Akhil Reed Amar, *The Bill of Rights: Creation and Reconstruction* (New Haven: Yale University Press, 1998).

For books used in this essay, the following were especially good on English antecedents as well as the American Revolution and its aftermath: Forrest McDonald, *Novus Ordo Seclorum: The Intellectual Origins of the Constitution* (Lawrence: University of Kansas Press, 1985); Leonard W. Levy, *Origins of the Bill of Rights* (New Haven: Yale University Press, 1999); and Robert Allen Rutland, *The Birth of the Bill of Rights, 1776-1791* (Chapel Hill: University of North Carolina Press, 1955). It is also instructive to read Irving Brant, *The Bill of Rights: Its Origin and Meaning* (New York: Mentor Books, 1965). Bernard Bailyn, *The Ideological Origins of the American Revolution* (Cambridge: Harvard University Press, 1967) is the most thorough analysis of the ideas and literature in the "pamphlet war" preceding our Revolution. To understand the formation of constitutions in the states and nation during the Revolutionary era, the best guide is still Gordon S. Wood, *The Creation of the American Republic, 1776-1787* (Chapel Hill: University of North Carolina Press, 1969). Note that Leonard W. Levy has written a great deal on freedom of the press—some of it challenged by other scholars. His title listed above is the most recent statement of his views and takes into account those of some of his critics.

On the contest between Federalists and Democratic-Republicans in the 1790s, the best guide is Stanley Elkins and Eric McKitrick, *The Age of Federalism: The Early American Republic, 1788-1800* (New York: Oxford University Press, 1993). The classic work on the Alien and Sedition Acts is James Morton Smith, *Freedom's Fetters: The Alien and Sedition Acts and American Civil Liberties* (Ithaca, N.Y.: Cornell University Press, 1956). Helpful in understanding the vital role of Anti-Federalists is Saul Cornell, *The Other Founders: Antifederalism and the Dissenting Tradition in America, 1788-1828* (Chapel Hill: University of North Carolina Press, 1999).

There is a variety of useful guides to exploring the courts and the Bill of Rights from 1791 on. Especially good is the book by Akhil Reed Amar already listed. Two others that helped were Harold L. Nelson, ed., *Freedom of the Press from Hamilton to the Warren Court* (Indianapolis: Bobbs-Merrill Co., 1967) and John R. Vile, *A Companion to the U.S. Constitution and Its Amendments* (Westport, Conn.: Praeger, 4th edition, 2006).

A Wilmington police officer reads the invaluable document assigned to her care during the tour stop at the Louise Wells Cameron Art Museum in March 2007. Image courtesy of the State Archives, N.C. Office of Archives and History, Raleigh.

"FREEDOM OF RELIGION": NORTH CAROLINA AND THE FIRST AMENDMENT

By Alan D. Watson

EDITOR'S NOTE: Dr. Alan D. Watson has written extensively on North Carolina history, utilizing the resources of the North Carolina State Archives, particularly the county court records, as thoroughly as any living historian. A native of Rocky Mount, he earned a B.A. degree in economics from Duke University in 1964, an M.A. in history from East Carolina College in 1966, and a Ph.D. in history from the University of South Carolina in 1971. He has served as a professor of history at the University of North Carolina at Wilmington since 1971. His publications include histories of Bertie, Edgecombe, Onslow, and Perquimans counties (all published by the Office of Archives and History); *Society in Colonial North Carolina* (1975, 1996); *A History of New Bern and Craven County* (1987); *Wilmington: Port of North Carolina* (1992); *Internal Improvements in Antebellum North Carolina* (2002); and *Bath: The First Town in North Carolina* (2005). He has also edited *Society in Early North Carolina: A Documentary History* (2000) and *African Americans in Early North Carolina: A Documentary History* (2005), both published by the Historical Publications Section. His articles have appeared in the *North Carolina Historical Review*, *South Carolina Historical Magazine*, *William and Mary Quarterly*, *South Atlantic Quarterly*, and *Journal of Negro History*. Dr. Watson has served on the North Carolina Historical Commission, the North Carolina National Register Advisory Committee, and the North Carolina Highway Historical Marker Advisory Committee. In 1998, he received the Christopher Crittenden Memorial Award from the North Carolina Literary and Historical Association, recognizing his lifetime contributions to the preservation of state history. Dr. Watson presented the following lecture at the Louise Wells Cameron Art Museum in Wilmington on March 9, 2007.

During the American Civil War, the Confederacy, the South, or rebellious element of the United States—the characterization depending upon the predisposition of the contemporary, historian, or present observer—constituted not only a battleground but also a treasure trove, at least for the victorious United States. In Craven County, North Carolina, after the fall of New Bern in March 1862, Northern soldiers apparently conducted themselves with some propriety in the town but ravaged the countryside. Edward Stanly, appointed military governor of the Union-occupied eastern coastal area of the state by President Abraham Lincoln, accused his own soldiers of plundering. In the words of another contemporary, Federal raids "nearly cleaned the county" of valuables, including a blooded horse worth $4,000, which was "found, trophied, and taken North."[1] Raleigh similarly suffered misfortune when Sherman's troops took control of the capital in 1865. Last year a legal treatise, published in 1708 and likely donated to the North Carolina Supreme Court in 1853, was returned to the

---

[1] Alan D. Watson, *A History of New Bern and Craven County* (New Bern, N.C.: Tryon Palace Commission, 1987), 391.

state after an absence of 141 years by an Indiana university librarian. On the title page reads the inscription, "Obtained in July 1865 at Raleigh North Carolina."[2]

Arguably the most valuable object sequestered by the Union soldiers was the North Carolina copy of the Bill of Rights. Even before the Fayetteville Convention in November 1789 ratified the federal Constitution, thereby making North Carolina the twelfth state in the Union, President George Washington had transmitted a copy of the proposed amendments to the Constitution to the governor of North Carolina. After the state approved the Constitution, the legislature in turn quickly ratified the amendments, ten of which became the Bill of Rights in 1791. The state's copy of the Bill of Rights apparently remained in the office of the secretary of state. When United States troops entered Raleigh in mid-April 1865 near the end of the Civil War, the State Capitol and its contents were in a state of disarray. At that juncture the Bill of Rights took flight.

Thirty-two years later, an article in an Indianapolis, Indiana, newspaper revealed the identity of the owner of the Bill of Rights, a man who had purchased it from a Union soldier for five dollars, and the saga of the Bill of Rights began. Though offered the opportunity to purchase the Bill of Rights early in the twentieth century and again in 1995, the State of North Carolina refused to buy its own, stolen property (whose value had risen from $5 in 1865 to $2 million latterly, a tidy appreciation even accounting for inflation). Subsequently the FBI seized the document in a sting operation in Philadelphia in 2003, and the legal contest for ownership of the Bill of Rights was joined. After the wheels of justice ground at their customary leisurely pace, the State of North Carolina finally has possession of its Bill of Rights. Still, the state awaits a final declaratory judgment from the federal judiciary to affirm its ownership of the document. Meanwhile, the Bill of Rights travels throughout North Carolina as further vindication of the state's claim to its history.

The protections granted by the Bill of Rights are familiar, beginning with the First Amendment—"Congress shall make no law respecting the establishment of religion, or prohibiting the free exercise thereof; or abridging the freedom of speech, or of the press; or the right of the people peaceably to assemble, and to petition the Government for a redress of grievances." Subsequent amendments address bearing arms, quartering soldiers, search and seizure, double jeopardy, speedy and public trial, jury trial, excessive bail, and cruel and unusual punishment. Lastly, the Tenth Amendment declares, "The powers not delegated to the United States by the Constitution, nor prohibited by it to the States, are reserved to the States respectively, or to the people," seemingly the foundation of the states' rights argument that led, ironically, to the defeat of the Confederacy and the loss of North Carolina's copy of the Bill of Rights. The states' rights theories, at least those of John C. Calhoun and other antebellum politicians, may have been discredited by the Civil War, but the essence of the remaining amendments, designed to protect the rights of individuals, remains vibrant—and

---

[2] *News and Observer* (Raleigh, N.C.), September 21, 2006.

controversial, including that part of the First Amendment "respecting the establishment of religion" and the "free exercise thereof," which is the subject of this address.

Although technically an adjunct of the federal Constitution of the United States, constituting as it did ten amendments to the original frame of government, the Bill of Rights actually proceeded from the deliberations over the ratification of the Constitution, and therefore might properly be deemed an extension of the original document. In the process of ratification, North Carolina played a consequential role in urging protections for individuals and states. But, of course, the antecedents of the "rights," including "freedom of religion," and the rationale for the perceived need for amendments ultimately lay in the history of the English colonies in North America, including North Carolina.

The settlement of that area of colonial English America that became the United States proceeded in part, originally in large part, from the desire of Europeans to escape an established or state-supported church and its attendant compulsion, if not persecution. At the dawn of the modern era in the Western world, the time of the voyages of Columbus, Western Europe exhibited a monolithic religious institution—the Roman Catholic Church. It was the established church to which all owed allegiance in the form of gifts and attendance. The Protestant Reformation, inadvertently initiated by Martin Luther, broke the stranglehold of Catholicism, leaving the Church still predominant in Portugal, Spain, France, and areas of Germanic Europe, but producing various Protestant sectaries elsewhere on the Continent. England was an anomaly, for the break with Rome and the creation of the nominally Protestant church, the Church of England or Anglican Church, proceeded from the marital travails of King Henry VIII. Nonetheless, the Anglican Church became the state church in England only a half century before the English seriously considered colonization in America.

However, within the Church of England were dissidents whose numbers and vociferousness increased with the passing years. Having found fault with the Catholic Church, they transferred their criticism to the Church of England, whose doctrines and practices greatly resembled those of the Catholic Church. The opposition, who came to be called Puritans—a broad term encompassing varied ideas of ecclesiastical matters—felt increasing pressure to conform to the Anglican Church. As England under Elizabeth I in the late sixteenth century evidenced interest in colonizing lands in North America, some Puritans may have sensed an opportunity to use overseas settlements as places to which to escape. Possibly Walter Raleigh's second colony, the famous Lost Colony, led by Gov. John White, represented the first attempt by Puritans to flee England to find refuge in America.

Whether or not the Lost Colony represented a Puritan project, the desire of religious dissidents in England to escape persecution constituted one of the principal motives for the early English settlement of America. The oft-told tale of the Pilgrims, a branch of the multifarious Puritans, quickly comes to mind. After an unsuccessful venture to Holland, William Bradford, John Alden, Priscilla Mullins, along with other Pilgrims and non-Pilgrims alike, sailed on board the *Mayflower* to Plymouth in present-day Massachusetts. The Plymouth colony was just the vanguard of a vast outpouring of Puritans that commenced in the late 1620s. Upon the accession of Charles I to the throne of England in 1625, the king and the archbishop of London instituted a determined policy of forcing the Puritans in England to observe the tenets of the Anglican Church, resulting in widespread persecution of nonconformists. The 1630s, informally known as the decade of the great Puritan migration, witnessed the departure of thousands of Puritans for the New World. Many sought refuge in the English West Indian islands, but substantial numbers made their way to New England—Massachusetts, Connecticut, and New Haven—as well as to Virginia and Maryland, though by mid-century the Puritan presence had mostly disappeared from the Chesapeake colonies.

Simultaneously with the departure of the Puritans from England, George and Cecil Calvert, father and son, prepared the colony of Maryland as a haven for another group of religiously oppressed peoples—Roman Catholics. In England, Catholics suffered political and civil disabilities because of their faith, which was associated with Spain and France, traditional enemies of England. Ironically, Protestants outnumbered Catholics in Maryland from the outset, and Cecil Calvert initially resorted to an undeclared policy of toleration for Christians in his province. The brief ascendancy of Puritans in England, the result of the Puritan revolution and Oliver Cromwell, prompted Calvert in 1649 to require his colony to accept legislation called the Act of Toleration that was designed to formalize his previously understood policy of tolerance. The statute called for the acceptance of all who believed in the Trinity—that is, Christians. Coincidentally, a few months later in the same year, the province of Maine to the far north enacted similar legislation.

Later in the seventeenth century, William Penn the Younger, an Anglican converted to the Society of Friends, sought to make Pennsylvania a refuge in America for Quakers. Founded in England by George Fox about 1650, the Society of Friends initially included adherents who had a thirst for martyrdom as well as a penchant for running through the streets on the Sabbath and disrupting the religious services of others. Although a bit more sedate, Penn spent time in an English jail for advocating his religious beliefs too strongly. Subsequently he prevailed upon King Charles II for a proprietary grant called Pennsylvania to be used as an asylum not only for Quakers in England but also for oppressed peoples "of all sorts of nations & perswasions." Quickly Penn and his government attempted to establish "a holy experiment," whereby anyone who believed in "one Almighty God" and who lived peaceably under the civil government of the colony might enjoy full religious liberty.[3]

In addition to Puritans, Catholics, and Quakers, English North America welcomed other harassed sectarians, including Scotch-Irish Presbyterians,

---

[3] John K. Alexander, "Pennsylvania: Pioneer in Safeguarding Personal Rights," in *The Bill of Rights and the States: The Colonial and Revolutionary Origins of American Liberties*, ed. by Patrick T. Conley and John P. Kaminski (Madison, Wis.: Madison House, 1992), 311, 312.

German Protestants, and French Protestants, or Huguenots. Scotch-Irish and Germans appeared in large numbers in the early eighteenth century. The proud, haughty, and pugnacious Scotch-Irish, Presbyterians to the core, began to depart their adopted country in part because of the Test Act passed by the English Parliament in 1704. That legislation excluded Presbyterians from civil and military offices, established the Anglican Church, denied the validity of Presbyterian marriage rites, and required Anglican services for funerals. Religious persecution on the Continent, conjoined with poverty, a seemingly endless series of wars, and strikingly cold winters, impelled the emigration of Protestant Germans to the English New World to escape their Catholic tormenters. Numerous pietistic sectaries, most notably perhaps the Moravians, augmented the numbers of Lutherans and German Reformed. After King Louis XIV of France revoked the Edict of Nantes in 1685, a decree that had offered toleration to French Protestants for more than three-quarters of a century, Huguenots began to leave predominantly Catholic France to go to England and America. Prominent early American names document the presence of the Huguenots—Revere and Faneuil in Boston, Jay and De Lancey in New York, and Manigault and Laurens in Charleston, South Carolina.

North Carolina offered sanctuary to a host of religious sectaries, the result in part of a policy of tolerance initiated by the Lords Proprietors, early owners of the colony, and continued later by the Crown of England. Quakers, immediately prominent in the Albemarle region and later in the Guilford County area, constituted the first element of organized religion in North Carolina. George Fox, founder of the Society of Friends, visited the colony briefly in 1672. Later Scotch-Irish and Scot Presbyterians, Baptists, Lutherans, German Reformed, Moravians, and Dunkers added to the list of dissenters in North Carolina. In 1765, acting governor William Tryon observed, "Every Sect of Religion abounds here (North Carolina), except the Roman Catholic."[4] Though they may not have "abounded," Catholics in fact were present, as attested by the execution of one of their number in New Bern in 1752 for counterfeiting. Methodists joined the ranks of the dissenters in North Carolina in the early 1770s. The Reverend Joseph Pilmore, probably the first Methodist minister to preach in North Carolina, visited Wilmington twice in 1773.

While it might appear that English America and North Carolina were havens for the oppressed—and to a degree they were, especially when compared to the European continent and England—nonetheless the various sectaries in the colonies usually encountered some degree of governmental restriction or coercion. Pennsylvania-Delaware under the influence of the Penn family and Rhode Island constituted exceptions. Roger Williams, banished from Massachusetts in part because of his objection to the close relationship between the civil authority and the Puritan Congregational Church, established a government in

---

[4] William S. Powell, ed., *The Correspondence of William Tryon and Other Selected Papers*, 2 vols. (Raleigh: Division of Archives and History, Department of Cultural Resources, 1980, 1981), 1:144.

The face of the "establishment" church in North Carolina. Built in 1734, St. Thomas Episcopal Church in Bath is the oldest surviving church building in the state. Image courtesy of the State Archives, N.C. Office of Archives and History, Raleigh.

Rhode Island that exercised power "only in civil things." Later the colony obtained formal recognition from King Charles II, who issued a royal charter in 1663 that declared that no one in Rhode Island should be "molested, punished, disquieted, or called into question for any differences in opinione in matters of religion."[5] Thus Rhode Island may have been the first government in modern Christendom to approximate the principle of religious freedom in practice.

Elsewhere, however, two church establishments—the Congregational Church in Puritan New England and the Church of England in the southern provinces—evoked the ire of non-establishment dissenters. By law the establishments in the affected colonies were able to collect taxes from all persons to support the favored churches. Ironically, the Puritans, who arrived in Massachusetts and Plymouth, never intended to separate church and state. In fact, in America they became the persecutors of nonconformists—exemplified by the

---

[5] Patrick T. Conley, "Rhode Island: Laboratory for the 'Lively Experiment,' " in Conley and Kaminski, *Bill of Rights and the States*, 130.

execution of four Quakers in Massachusetts—before King Charles II demanded some measure of tolerance in the colony. To the south, the Church of England became the established church in Virginia, North and South Carolina, and Georgia. As a result, those who had fled establishments in England and Europe often confronted similar constraints in America.

In North Carolina the Anglican establishment supported by English authority helped to feed the many grievances that led ultimately to the American Revolution. Toleration for non-Anglicans or dissenters, except Roman Catholics, who were proscribed from the outset, and Jews, who were too few to arouse concern, was grudging. Dissenters with whom the established church had to deal were deemed nuisances at best. Surveying his parish, Anglican priest James Reed in New Bern observed, "the [A]nabaptist are obstinate, illiterate & grossly ignorant, the Methodist, ignorant, censorious & uncharitable, [and] the Quakers, Rigid, but the Presbyterians are pretty moderate except here & there a bigot or rigid Calvinist."[6] Of the non-Anglicans, only Presbyterian ministers were permitted to perform marriage rites and that not until 1766. Dissenting clergy might teach school only if they agreed not to oppose the doctrine and liturgy of the established church.

Clearly the realization of toleration in matters of conscience had yet to be achieved before the war for independence. However, the spirit of liberation embodied by the American Revolution not only breached the walls of political and economic restraints in the colonies but also embraced other areas of life, including the abolition of slavery and freedom of religion. Thomas Jefferson in the Declaration of Independence represented the feeling of many when he stated that government should be founded on such principles and given such powers as "shall seem most likely to effect . . . [the] Safety and Happiness" of the people. For inspiration, Jefferson drew upon fellow Virginian George Mason's famous Bill of Rights, which accompanied the Virginia state constitution of June 1776. Nonetheless, in the Declaration of Independence, Jefferson approached the subject of religion obliquely, never mentioning the Anglican establishment in the colonies in his manifold criticisms of King George III in the document.[7]

In his Bill of Rights, however, Mason claimed that "religion, or the duty which we owe to our Creator, and the manner of discharging it, can be directed only by reason and conviction, not by force or violence; and therefore all men are equally entitled to the free exercise of religion, according to the dictates of conscience."[8] In December 1776, six months after Virginia adopted its constitution, North Carolina held a convention for the same purpose. Article 19 of the Declaration of Rights that accompanied the North Carolina Constitution stated Mason's

6 William L. Saunders, ed., *The Colonial Records of North Carolina*, 10 vols. (Raleigh: State of North Carolina, 1886-1890), 6:265.

7 Henry Steele Commager, ed., *Documents of American History*, 2 vols. (New York: Appleton-Century-Crofts, 1963), 1:100.

8 Commager, *Documents of American History*, 1:104.

proposition more succinctly: "all men have a natural and unalienable right to worship Almighty God according to the dictates of their own conscience."[9] North Carolinians appreciated Mason's conviction but actually appropriated their language from the Pennsylvania Declaration of Rights.

The revolutionary spirit led not only to a more determined policy of tolerance but also to the disestablishment of the Church of England in the southern states. Conforming to its Declaration of Rights, Section 34 of North Carolina's state constitution renounced the Anglican establishment. It forbade elevating any church or denomination in preference to another, enforcing any person "on any pretense whatsoever" to attend any place of worship, and taxing anyone for the support of any church or minister. Rather, "all persons [were] at liberty to exercise their own mode of worship."[10] After three-quarters of a century, dissenters in North Carolina exchanged their discriminatory status for a measure of ecclesiastical equality.

The North Carolina Constitution further sought to separate civil and religious spheres. Section 31 prohibited clergymen from serving in the legislature while they exercised pastoral functions. Not only did that stipulation prevent an overlapping of secular and spiritual authority in the legislature but it also avoided the potential misuse of informal deference granted to ministers of the gospel. The constitution also permitted clergymen of all denominations to perform marriages, a prerogative formerly reserved to Anglicans and Presbyterians. Last, during those trying times of revolution, Section 34 pointedly observed that ministers who espoused "treasonable or seditious discourses" were not exempt from legal trial and punishment.[11]

Most states emulated North Carolina in opting for the free exercise of religious sentiments. That end was achieved either by a constitution—in Virginia, Georgia, New Jersey, New York, and South Carolina—or a declaration or bill of rights—in Pennsylvania, Delaware, Maryland, Massachusetts, and New Hampshire. Virginia was the last of the southern states to disestablish the Church of England, which became the Protestant Episcopal Church of America following the Revolution. A combination of taxpayers, evangelicals, and secularist politicians led by James Madison pressured the House of Burgesses in 1786 into approving the Statute of Religious Freedom, which earlier had been written by Thomas Jefferson. That law, a model statement of separation of church and state, read: "no man shall be compelled to frequent or support any religious worship, place or ministry whatsoever, nor shall be enforced, restrained, molested, or burthened in his body or goods, nor shall otherwise suffer on account of his religious opinions or belief; but that all men shall be free to profess,

[9] John L. Cheney, ed., *North Carolina Government, 1585-1979: A Narrative and Statistical History* (Raleigh: North Carolina Department of the Secretary of State, 1981), 810.
[10] Cheney, *North Carolina Government*, 814-815.
[11] Cheney, *North Carolina Government*, 815.

and by argument to maintain, their opinion in matters of religion, and that the same shall in no wise diminish, enlarge or affect their civil capacities."[12]

Meanwhile, as the former English colonies set about to win the independence that they had so audaciously declared, they also undertook the drafting of a constitution to transform thirteen separate political entities into a formal nation. The result, the Articles of Confederation, established a most tenuous union, a mere shell of a national government. The states, none more so than North Carolina, being exceedingly jealous of their autonomy, protective of individual rights, and fearful of executive (British) authority for more than a century, understandably created a politically weak national association of thirteen virtually independent states. At that, North Carolina only reluctantly accepted the new Constitution.

The Articles of Confederation reflected the spirit of freedom and equalitarianism inherent in the movement for independence as well as a studied concern for the rights of the states and their citizens. As in North Carolina, protections for those valued rights, whether freedom of conscience, trial by jury, or freedom of the press, were embodied in state constitutions and accompanying bills of rights. A national bill of rights proved unnecessary, for the Confederation government never threatened the fundamental liberties for which the colonials had fought and won a revolution. As a result, however, the Articles of Confederation had created a central authority so weak that it embarrassed some Americans by its ineptitude in foreign affairs and frightened others by its inability to protect property interests and promote sound economic policies at home. George Washington represented the view of many when he privately opined, "We are fast verging to anarchy and confusion!"[13]

Immediately upon the implementation of the Articles of Confederation in 1781, efforts were made to strengthen the authority of the national government. Other than Rhode Island, no state was more skeptical of those intentions than North Carolina, for the bulk of Carolinians—relatively poor, scattered farmers—appreciated the protections guaranteed by the state constitution and looked askance upon a distant, powerful, threatening national government. Still, in 1787, the so-called Founding Fathers produced the federal Constitution that promised to reverse the power relationship between states and nation. The proposed new government represented a potential threat to the rights of the states and the people therein, but after a contentious struggle, the requisite number of states approved the new constitution to make it operational in 1789.

North Carolina remained apart from the new nation. In a convention that met in Hillsborough in 1788 to consider the ratification of the Constitution, opponents of the new government, called Anti-Federalists, held a decisive edge. They feared the power of a central authority and argued for amendments to

[12] Commager, *Documents of American History*, 1:126.
[13] Quoted in Richard B. Morris, "The Confederation Period and the American Historian," *William and Mary Quarterly*, 3rd Series, 13 (April 1956): 140.

protect state and individual rights. Proponents of the Constitution, called Federalists, rejected the need for such protections. They noted that amendments did not accompany the Articles of Confederation, to which the the Anti-Federalists responded, the Articles government posed no threat to the states or the people. Federalists also contended that the powers of the national government were too well defined to require restrictions, a proposition to which Anti-Federalists took adamant exception. Finally, the Federalists claimed that any enumeration of some rights would inevitably overlook others, implying their inherence in the national government. The Anti-Federalists disagreed with that somewhat specious logic.

Thus North Carolina failed to ratify the Constitution at the Hillsborough Convention. The Anti-Federalists hoped that the reticence of the state would pressure the new nation into accepting amendments to the Constitution. In fact, the Hillsborough Convention proposed several amendments that were designed to check federal power and ensure states rights, as well as a declaration (or bill) of rights that would secure personal liberties. The declaration of rights included many of the guarantees that accompanied the North Carolina state constitution. After addressing such fundamentals as due process of law, trial by jury, excessive bail, cruel and unusual punishment, freedom of speech and assembly, and the right to bear arms, the list concluded with the following: "all men have an equal, natural and unalienable right to the free exercise of religion, according to the dictates of conscience, and that no particular religion, sect or society ought to be favored or established by law in preference to others."[14]

The failure of the Hillsborough Convention to ratify the Constitution in effect left North Carolina outside of the Union when the United States government organized in April 1789. However, the pressure from North Carolina, in conjunction with similar demands for limitations on the national government from other states, proved fruitful. Immediately Congress began to collect and codify proposals for amendments to the Constitution that were transmitted to the states before the end of the year. Satisfied, North Carolina held a second convention at Fayetteville in November 1789 and opted to join the new nation. Quickly the state legislature voted to approve a list of amendments that became the national Bill of Rights, an action in which most North Carolinians must have taken some comfort. As Anti-Federalist Joseph McDowell had said earlier in Hillsborough, "I know the necessity for a federal government. I therefore wish this was one in which our liberties and privileges were secured; . . . A bill of rights ought to have been inserted, to ascertain our most valuable and unalienable rights."[15]

[14] Walter Clark, ed., *The State Records of North Carolina*, 16 vols. (11-26) (Winston and Goldsboro, N.C.: State of North Carolina, 1895-1906), 22:19.

[15] Jonathan Elliot, *The Debates in the Several State Conventions on the Adoption of the Federal Constitution as Recommended by the General Convention at Philadelphia in 1787*, 5 vols., 2nd ed. (New York: Burt Franklin, 1968), 4:210.

Thus North Carolina played a conspicuous role in the realization of the Bill of Rights, including the clause respecting "freedom of religion." But wait. There is an epilogue. Colonial North Carolina, like most of the English provinces, discriminated against Roman Catholics and Jews, few in number as they were, by denying them the right to hold public office. The state constitution of 1776 formalized that policy, and later some Anti-Federalists wanted to apply that ban by amendment to the United States government. But Congress rejected a Protestant religious test. Later, in 1835 and 1861, North Carolina eliminated civil disabilities against Catholics and Jews, respectively. In so doing, the state came to agree with James Iredell, one of its foremost revolutionaries and its first representative on the United States Supreme Court, who had said in the Hillsborough convention in 1788, "This country has already had the honor of setting an example of civil freedom, and I trust it will likewise have the honor of teaching the rest of the world the way to religious freedom also."[16]

SUGGESTED READINGS

Antieau, Chester James, Arthur T. Downey, and Edward C. Roberts. *Freedom from Federal Establishment: Formation and Early History of the First Amendment Religion Clauses*. Milwaukee: Bruce Publishing Company, 1964.

Conley, Patrick T. and John P. Kaminski, eds. *The Bill of Rights and the States: The Colonial and Revolutionary Origins of American Liberties*. Madison, Wis.: Madison House, 1992.

Conser, Walter H., Jr. *A Coat of Many Colors: Religion and Society along the Cape Fear River of North Carolina*. Lexington: University Press of Kentucky, 2006.

Curry, Thomas J. *The First Freedoms: Church and State in America to the Passage of the First Amendment*. New York: Oxford University Press, 1986.

Morgan, Robert J. *James Madison on the Constitution and the Bill of Rights*. New York; Westport, Conn.; London: Greenwood Press, 1988.

Rutland, Robert. *The Birth of the Bill of Rights*. Chapel Hill: University of North Carolina Press, 1955.

Sweet, William Warren. *Religion in Colonial America*. New York: Cooper Square Publishers, 1965.

[16] Elliot, *Debates*, 4:196.

A school group enters the 1767 Chowan County Courthouse to view the Bill of Rights in April 2007. Image courtesy of the State Archives, N.C. Office of Archives and History, Raleigh.

THE FIRST AMENDMENT RIGHT OF FREEDOM OF SPEECH IN THE TWENTY-FIRST CENTURY

By Freddie L. Parker

EDITOR'S NOTE: Dr. Freddie L. Parker earned B.A. and M.A. degrees from North Carolina Central University and a Ph.D. from Duke University. He has been on the faculty at North Carolina Central University since 1976 and currently serves as chair of the history department. In 2001, he was appointed to the North Carolina Historical Commission. Dr. Parker is the author of two monographs: *Running for Freedom: Slave Runaways in North Carolina, 1775-1840* (1993); and *Stealing a Little Freedom: Advertisements for Slave Runaways in North Carolina, 1791-1840* (1994). He gave these remarks on April 20, 2007, at the restored Chowan County Courthouse in Edenton.

I am happy to have this opportunity this evening to be with you on this tour of the Bill of Rights, North Carolina's copy of this magnificent document, a document taken from the people of North Carolina at the close of the Civil War. After a long, tedious journey of more than 140 years, this original document has found its way back home. For the people of North Carolina, and especially for those of us who are concerned with historic preservation, archives, and archaeology, this is indeed a glorious time.

I want to share with you my thoughts on the First Amendment to the Bill of Rights. The First Amendment contains five guarantees—freedom of religion, freedom of speech, freedom of the press, freedom of assembly, and a redress of grievances. I will talk briefly this evening about freedom of speech.

North Carolina was one of those colonies that held out ratifying the Constitution for a number of reasons. But the fact that there was no bill of rights was a primary reason. When delegates (184 Anti-Federalists and 84 Federalists) met in Hillsborough to consider ratification of the Constitution, opponents of ratification—the Anti-Federalists—walked away with a victory. The vote was 184 against ratification, 84 for ratification. In November 1789, North Carolina voted to ratify the Constitution, but only after the Bill of Rights had been proposed.

Over the past two weeks, the airways have been inundated with the Don Imus affair. Don Imus has used his radio program and, more recently, MSNBC as a "shock jock." He has ridiculed folks, used inflammatory language, and generally said what he wanted to say without reprisal. When lambasted for what some believe to be crude language, he and others who defend him have turned to the First Amendment. "I can say what I want to say" appears to be the attitude that so many of us assume, and we quickly point to the First Amendment to support that claim. At the same time, rap artists have been taken to task for the "offensive lyrics" in their songs. They have been defended by "free speech" advocates, attorneys, people who buy their music, and record producers and companies who stand to make millions of dollars. So-called bad words sell. These recent developments clearly show us that the two-hundred-year-old debate over free speech will continue, and that the courts will continue to hear cases and interpret and reinterpret this important amendment to the United States Constitution. The most important thing is that this freedom exists in the Constitution.

There is a long history, a legacy of this notion of free speech, from Socrates to the Magna Carta of 1215, to Erasmus, to John Milton in 1644, to the English Bill of Rights in 1689, to the Declaration of the Rights of Man in 1789, a document central to the French Revolution. I believe that the framers of the Constitution would be surprised and perhaps alarmed today by the mounds of litigation on court dockets across the United States with regard to free speech. The framers might be shocked by the enormous list of why a particular act is a violation of the First Amendment. Relative to our busy, technologically advanced world today, life was rather simple when the framers met in Philadelphia, Pennsylvania, in 1787 to draft what would be our present Constitution. According to the first U.S. census in 1790, there were about 4,000,000 people in the United States, nearly one-fourth of whom were slaves scattered throughout the North and the South. Contrast that with a present-day population of nearly 302,000,000. We live in a more complex world, a world that has increased our umbrella of what is protected by the First Amendment.

When one looks at the landscape of Supreme Court cases just in the past fifteen years, we find that some laws that might have limited free speech in certain ways were overturned by the high court. In *Ashcroft v. Free Speech Coalition* (2002), the Court ruled that the federal 1996 Child Pornography Act went too far by including "virtual child pornography" and computer-generated images as forms of pornography. The majority opinion pointed out that under overly broad or vague definitions of child pornography Shakespeare's *Romeo and Juliet* might be banned. In *Lamb's Chapel v. Center Moriches Union Free School District* (1993), the Supreme Court rejected a New York school district's decision to refuse to allow school property to be used for religious-oriented programs. The Court decided that to refuse the use of public facilities to a religious group favors some viewpoints to the disadvantage of others. In contrast to those two decisions, however, the Supreme Court decided in the case of *Hill v. Colorado* (2000) that the right to free speech was not violated when protesters were prohibited from coming within eight feet of a person. The case concerned demonstrations at abortion clinics. The Colorado statute, the Court determined, did not prevent demonstrators from yelling, holding signs, or distributing literature with the permission of willing recipients.

All of us have become accustomed to watching the dozens of cable channels. But that industry carries speech, according to Congress and the U.S. Supreme Court, and over the past ten years, it has brought suit against the Federal Communications Commission for legislation and policy that allegedly infringed upon free speech. In a recent case, *Turner Broadcasting v. the FCC*, the Supreme Court ruled in favor of the cable industry in its quest to carry programming into the homes of millions of Americans. The Court has walked the thin line of what is and what is not protected under the First Amendment.

Freddie L. Parker addresses the audience in the courtroom of the renovated colonial courthouse in Edenton on April 20, 2007. Image courtesy of the State Archives, N.C. Office of Archives and History, Raleigh.

Ten years ago the Supreme Court ruled that it was a violation of free speech for states to prohibit the advertising of alcoholic beverage retail prices. In 2002, the Court struck down a town ordinance demanding that Jehovah's Witnesses register with the mayor and receive a permit before going door to door to distribute the *Watchtower* and other publications. The Court has heard cases from university and college students demanding that they no longer pay fees that support ideological or political speech. In 2000, the Court reversed a lower court decision and stated emphatically that students' fees should not support speech that does not support the "viewpoint neutrality principle."

As litigation continues, and as we all walk the tightrope of limitations on what we can say, the First Amendment will continue to be a vital part of American political discourse.

Dick Lankford (*center, rear*), state archivist of North Carolina, accompanied the Bill of Rights to all of its tour stops, beginning at the Airborne and Special Operations Museum in Fayetteville in February 2007. Image courtesy of the State Archives, N.C. Office of Archives and History, Raleigh.

THE BILL OF RIGHTS: ITS ORIGINS, ORIGINALS, AND ODYSSEYS

By Charlene Bangs Bickford

EDITOR'S NOTE: Charlene Bangs Bickford is coeditor and project director of the First Federal Congress Project at George Washington University, where since 1967 she has helped edit the *Documentary History of the First Federal Congress, 1789-1791*. She earned a B.A. degree from St. Lawrence University in 1966 and an M.A. in history from George Washington University in 1969. She coauthored (with Kenneth R. Bowling) *Birth of the Nation: The First Federal Congress, 1789-1791* (1989), and coedited *Creating the Bill of Rights: The Documentary Record from the First Federal Congress* (1991). Bickford has written articles concerning the First Federal Congress that have appeared in the *Journal of the Early Republic*; *This Constitution*; *Prologue: the Journal of the National Archives*; *and Manuscripts*. She has also contributed articles to *The Blessings of Liberty: Bicentennial Lectures at the National Archives* (1986); *Well Begun, Chronicles of the Early National Period* (1989); and *Inventing Congress: Origins and Establishment of the First Federal Congress* (1999). Bickford has been an active member of the Association for Documentary Editing (serving as secretary-treasurer in 1979 and president in 1986), the Society for History in the Federal Government (president-elect and president, 1990-1992), and the Organization of American Historians. She was the founder and coordinator of the Coalition to Save Our Documentary Heritage (1981-1987). She has served on the Virginia State Historical Records Advisory Board (1987-1992) and the Advisory Committee on Congressional Records (1991-1995). Bickford has participated in teacher-training institutes sponsored by the Library of Congress, the American Bar Association, and the National Endowment for the Humanities; taught a graduate-level historical documentary editing course for George Mason University and George Washington University; and served as lecturer and resident adviser at the Institute for the Editing of Historical Documents. She has received distinguished service awards from both the Association for Documentary Editing and the Society of American Archivists. She delivered these remarks at the North Carolina Museum of History in Raleigh on September 17, 2007.

Senators and representatives who made the journey to New York City during the late winter of 1789 to serve in the First Federal Congress understood that they faced daunting challenges. They had to act quickly to address the needs of the new nation and its people and demonstrate that a stable, energetic, and useful federal government was in place under the new Constitution, while also carefully working to preserve and strengthen the tenuous national unity. The awesome and immediate agenda that they faced included: establishing an adequate and workable system to provide for and collect the revenue necessary for the federal government to meet its expenses; defining the structure, jurisdiction, and procedures of the federal judiciary; determining which departments were necessary for the operation of the executive branch and establishing those entities; and providing for the national defense and protection of the American people, particularly the settlers on the frontiers.

This Congress faced the challenge of fleshing out the bare-bones structure outlined in the Constitution. Its every decision would be precedent setting, constant interpretation of the Constitution would be necessary, and every action would set the tone for or expand upon the framework of the new government. In addition, issues that related to the balance of power between the states and the federal government constantly arose. Virginia representative James Madison best captured the role of this Congress when he wrote to his father: "We are in a wilderness without a single footstep to guide us. It is consequently necessary to explore the way with great labour and caution." When one recognizes the organic nature of some of its most important and enduring legislation, such as the Judiciary Act of 1789, it is easy to see why contemporaries saw this Congress as a "second sitting of the Federal Convention."

In addition, two polarizing issues that had bedeviled the Confederation Congress could not be put off for long. The failure to fund the domestic and foreign indebtedness incurred to pay the expenses of the Revolutionary War, as well as the war debts of the states, was destabilizing to both the national and some state economies, causing unrest and endangering the new nation's international credit. Several confederation period attempts to establish a permanent seat of government had failed, while revealing sectional divisions and jealousies. Competition to become the much-coveted federal district was intense. The correspondence of members of the First Federal Congress, as well as the diary kept by Senator William Maclay of Pennsylvania, makes it clear that from the moment that members started to arrive in New York, more meetings of members in taverns, state caucuses on and off the floor, and impromptu negotiations on street corners centered around the location of the seat of government than any other question.

On top of this full and potentially divisive agenda, Congress was also charged with legislating the organization and operation of the entire federal government, including the 1790 census, copyright and patent regulations, a land office, a mint, a uniform militia system, and rules for naturalization of new citizens. It would receive more than six hundred petitions from citizens or groups seeking federal government relief or action. Thus, if only from the perspective of their work load, it is easy to understand members' utter lack of enthusiasm when, barely a month after the first House of Representatives attained a quorum, James Madison launched his quest to fulfill a campaign promise to his Virginia Piedmont-area constituents to seek amendments to the new Constitution.

The majority of members feared that Madison's efforts had the potential to endanger both the fragile unity that had been achieved and Congress's progress on its agenda. They had excellent reasons for not wanting to open this Pandora's box. A quick look back at the actions of the federal convention and the ratification process will reveal the source of those concerns.

The concept of protections for individual rights against a powerful government was well entrenched and developed in the American colonies, to which so many settlers had actually emigrated to escape oppressive governments in Europe. Thus, the detailed indictment of King George III contained in the Declaration of Independence made clear that Great Britain's infringement of these rights was intolerable and one of the prime causes for full-scale revolt aimed at separation from Great Britain.

In retrospect, therefore, it is difficult to understand why the founders at the federal convention, voting by state delegations, unanimously rejected a proposal from Elbridge Gerry of Massachusetts and Virginia delegate George Mason to add to the federal Constitution a bill of rights similar to those already in most state constitutions. Gerry and Mason recognized that such amendments could serve to relieve the public's apprehensions about the protection of the individual under a new federal government with substantially increased power. Unfortunately, their colleagues clearly did not want to consider this issue. Frustrated, Mason left the convention and went home to his Potomac River plantation; Gerry refused to sign the document because it lacked both a bill of rights and a call for a second convention to consider amendments.

The convention's decision, while expedient, clearly was ill considered and provided ammunition for opponents of the Constitution, who geared up to oppose this new governing document. Though there were gradations of opposition, two distinct groups emerged. First, there were those who would be satisfied with the addition of a clear listing of the individual rights that Americans had both fought for and endured hardships to secure. The second group was made up of those that strongly believed that the Constitution created a structure for an overly powerful national government that not only endangered the rights of individuals, but also threatened the powers of the thirteen sovereign states. This group sought significant alterations to the governmental structure and powers in the Constitution in addition to the protection of rights. It is clear that the absence of a bill of rights helped to stir popular opinion against the Constitution, while the leaders of the anti-ratification movement used it to bolster their campaign for substantial alterations to the constitutional framework.

In December 1787, state ratification conventions finally started to convene, and by the end of that year, Delaware and Georgia had ratified unanimously, while Pennsylvania Federalists had achieved a two-thirds majority. After Connecticut's January 9, 1788, ratification by a 128-to-40 majority, the process began to run into bumps in the road to ratification. The Massachusetts Convention ratified by a close vote of 187 to 168, and then only after it had attached nine proposed amendments, some of which would have protected individual rights, while others aimed at limiting the powers of the federal government.

A major blow was struck when a March 24 statewide referendum in Rhode Island failed by an overwhelming vote of 2,711 to 239. Though Rhode Island, the only state that did not send delegates to the federal convention, must be looked upon as a special case, it is tempting to speculate as to what might have happened if other states had offered their citizens an up-or-down vote through a referendum. There is good reason to believe that submission to the popular will could have derailed the ratification movement. Without a bill of rights, the citizenry at large was very suspicious of the document.

A month later, things were back on track, and the news was better when Maryland became the seventh state to ratify. The strategy of the Constitution's supporters in that state was to completely refrain from making supporting speeches or engaging their opponents in arguments. Instead they just sat and let the opponents have their say and then voted to ratify, 63 to 11. In May South Carolina ratified by a two-to-one margin, but not without adding this strong statement on behalf of state sovereignty and rights: "This Convention doth also declare that no Section or paragraph of the said Constitution warrants a Construction that the states do not retain every power not expressly relinquished by them and vested in the General Government of the Union"—a forceful precursor to the Tenth Amendment to the Constitution. Two months later, New Hampshire became the ninth state to ratify, but the vote was 57 to 47, and the convention proposed a list of amendments that was very similar to that of Massachusetts.

With New Hampshire's action, the Federalists could take satisfaction from having achieved the assent of the constitutionally required three-fourths of the states, and on July 2, the day that the Confederation Congress received official notification of New Hampshire's action, that body appointed a committee to report an act for putting the Constitution into effect. Nevertheless, supporters and opponents of the Constitution were well aware that the new government could certainly not succeed without the support of both Virginia and New York. Perhaps the old Congress had actually received unofficial word of Virginia's June 25 ratification when it appointed the committee. The Virginia vote was 89 to 79, after a bitterly contested three-week convention. Its ratification was agreed to with the submission of proposed changes, including not only a declaration of rights elucidated in twenty very detailed amendments, but also twenty substantive alterations to the Constitution itself. Virginia was also considering a call for a second convention.

On July 26, 1788, New York became the essential "Eleventh Pillar" in the federal edifice by a very narrow margin of 30 to 27. That state not only submitted the longest list of both rights amendments and substantive alterations to date, but also voted to send a circular letter out to the other states seeking a new convention. Then, on August 2, the first North Carolina convention proposed amendments to the Constitution but refused to ratify until amendments were submitted to Congress and a second constitutional convention was called. When the First Federal Congress began meeting the next spring, both North Carolina and Rhode Island remained out of the Union.

It is important to remember that during the roughly ten months between the conclusion of the federal convention and North Carolina's refusal to ratify, an enormous and wide-ranging public debate over the Constitution occupied the nation. Like modern-day political parties, Federalists and Anti-Federalists—we love to use Elbridge Gerry's terms and refer to these early groups as "Rats" and "Anti-Rats"—employed every method available to them to get their message into print and circulation. Just the pamphlets, newspaper pieces, political cartoons, poems, and letters that were circulated outside of their state of origin during this debate fill six volumes of the *Documentary History of the Ratification of the Constitution*. This output is truly amazing, particularly recognizing that these eighteenth-century propagandists were writing with quill pens by the light of candles or oil lamps. Although the "Rats" were the eventual winners of the ratification battle, it is clear that the longer it went on, the more the arguments of the "Anti-Rats," particularly those relating to individual and states rights, were resonating with the public.

James Madison earned the sobriquet, "Father of the Constitution," by virtue of drafting the Virginia Plan, which formed the blueprint for the Constitution, and for his role in adding a bill of rights to make the document more palatable to some of the states, including North Carolina, that were hesitant to adopt a federal constitution without guarantees of individual rights. Image courtesy of the State Archives, N.C. Office of Archives and History, Raleigh.

Therefore one might expect that a substantial number of opponents of the Constitution would have achieved success in the first federal elections, but this was not the case. During its first session, the First Federal Congress's membership included only two senators and eleven representatives that had opposed ratification. Certainly this block did not have the votes to succeed in an effort to amend the Constitution. They could draw attention to the amendments proposed by their states and agitate for action on them, but without support from the Federalists, such actions would be in vain.

With the Anti-Federalists nearly powerless in Congress, what was it that caused Madison, the man who was a key supporter of a strong central government at the federal convention, who had opposed the Gerry/Mason attempt to add a declaration of rights, and who worked as diligently as any Federalist for the Constitution's ratification, to change course and become the champion of the cause of amendments in the Congress? Congress had been meeting for a little over a month, but he was already the unofficial floor leader of the House of Representatives, and his close ties with the president added strength to his position. Why put that at risk?

Two major factors brought about Madison's conversion. The first was a transatlantic "conversation" that he had with his friend Thomas Jefferson on the issue. The second was the reality of Virginia electoral politics. The Virginia General Assembly, dominated by opponents of the Constitution led by the fiery Patrick Henry, rejected Madison and appointed Anti-Federalists Richard Henry Lee and William Grayson to the U.S. Senate. Then Henry and his allies drew a district that included some distinctly Anti-Federal counties, and Madison found himself opposed by his friend, Anti-Federalist James Monroe. Letters from supporters convinced him to return home from Philadelphia, where he was stopping on his way to serve in the Confederation Congress, in order to actively campaign for office. Thus, the two future presidents of the United States faced off in the most competitive congressional race in the country.

At the Virginia Convention, Madison had repeated the Federalist argument that a bill of rights was unnecessary, if not dangerous, and thus during the campaign Madison found himself accused of being absolutely opposed to any amendments to the Constitution. These accusations forced him to write letters to friends that were then published in the local papers. In the letters he committed himself to not just introducing but actively pushing for amendments. Making this promise was not difficult for him because he had become convinced that the Congress could convert most Anti-Federalists into supporters of the new government by proposing amendments that would protect individual rights and thus avoid a continuing battle over substantive alterations. The grueling and progressively more divisive ratification battle, the number of states that submitted proposed amendments, the calls for a second convention, and the refusal of two states to ratify all combined to convince this practical politician to become the champion of the cause of amending the Constitution. He even converted George Washington, convincing him to ask Congress to consider amendments to strengthen the "characteristic rights of freemen" in the inaugural address that Madison himself drafted for the general.

Madison's May 4, 1789, motion to consider amendments to the Constitution on May 25 was followed by Theodorick Bland's May 5 introduction of Virginia's application to Congress to call a second convention. Congress was immediately forced to find a way to handle this application while still paying proper respect to the Commonwealth of Virginia, though no other applications for a convention had been received. They voted to enter the application on the journal of the House before filing it in the clerk's office.

After another postponement, on June 8 Madison finally introduced his proposed amendments, which he believed should be interwoven into the body of the Constitution. They contain a much more extensive and very specific articulation of individual rights—particularly those relating to judicial proceedings—than the document that we honor today, as well as some alterations, including term limits for the president. One that was not rights related, the one on reserved powers that became the Tenth Amendment, significantly omitted the words "expressly" or "clearly." The omission of this word gutted the amendment and left the Constitution open to the doctrine of implied powers. Residents of the present-day District of Columbia would be happy to see that Madison proposed restrictions on Congress's exclusive jurisdiction over the federal district.

On June 21, when Madison again sought to have the whole House consider his proposals, Georgia's James Jackson moved to put off the discussion until March 1, 1790. Jackson used a nautical metaphor to protest considering amendments before the constitutional ship that had been constructed and fitted out could be tested on the seas of government. The compromise solution was to commit Madison's resolutions, along with all the amendments proposed by the states. The committee's July 28 report was an indicator of how far the majority of the House was willing to go. It substantially tightened Madison's proposed amendments, and while it did retain his suggested requirement for absolute separation of powers within the federal government, most of his other proposed alterations were dropped.

Researchers who explore the debates of the first House of Representatives search in vain for discussions of the meaning and original intent of those who passed the Bill of Rights. Unfortunately, though several reporters took notes and reported on the debates, virtually no discussions of this type exist. In fact, the most extensive recorded debates relate to whether or not to amend the Constitution at all, postponing this discussion until Congress had made more progress on its agenda, and adding a proposed amendment that would have specifically declared it as a power of the state legislatures to instruct their state's representatives and senators. Discerning original intent from the debates, or indeed from the letters that the members wrote, is an impossible task.

The respect in which Madison's House colleagues held him gradually won support for the amendments from other Federalists, but at a price. Before sending the amendments to the Senate, they made several changes to his proposals. Perhaps most significant among these, they refused to accept his wish to add to the Constitution's preamble an eloquent statement, based in part on the Declaration of Independence: that all power comes from the people; that government should be exercised for their benefit, which he defined as "the enjoyment of life and liberty, with the right of acquiring and using property, and generally of pursuing and obtaining happiness and safety"; and that the people retain the right to change a government whenever it was adverse to or inadequate for the purposes of its institutions.

While James Madison's persistent push for amendments in the First Federal Congress has earned him the title of Father of the Bill of Rights, we can thank Roger Sherman of Connecticut for the fact that we have a document that we can proudly point to as our Bill of Rights. During the House debate, Sherman was insistent that the body of the Constitution that he and his fellow delegates to the federal convention had signed and which had been ratified by the states should not be altered. Despite Madison's opposition, Sherman's arguments eventually prevailed in the House.

Senator William Maclay was absent with the gout for most of the period of the Senate's consideration of the amendments sent to them by the House. Thus, we know little about what happened except that the Senate did a substantial edit on the amendments. Most significantly, it eliminated language that prohibited Congress from infringing upon the rights of conscience, declared separation of powers as a principle of the United States Constitution, exempted from military service those with religious scruples, and forbade the states from abridging certain rights of Americans. Madison, who had been unhappy with the changes made by the House, was even more displeased by the changes made by the Senate. Senator Grayson of Virginia reported on the Senate's actions in a letter to Patrick Henry: "the lower house sent up amendments which held out a safeguard to personal liberty in a great many instances, but this disgusted the Senate, and though we made every exertion to save them, they are so mutilated & gutted that in fact they are good for nothing."

After more back-and-forth between the two houses relating to the numerous Senate changes, agreement was finally achieved. On September 28, 1789, the next to the last day of the first session, the Speaker of the House and the vice-president signed the handwritten copy of the twelve proposed amendments to the U.S. Constitution passed by Congress and certified correct by the Joint Committee on Enrolled Acts. On the same day, Congress agreed to a joint resolution directing President George Washington to send a copy of the proposed amendments to each state, including the two states not yet part of the Union. Because the president had no constitutional role in the amendment process, Washington did not sign these documents, but nevertheless, Congress clearly understood the political benefit to be gained from his playing the role of transmitter. As was true of the Constitution, his involvement provided a seal of approval from the most respected and revered person in the United States.

Of course Congress was anxious to use rights-related amendments to defuse at least a part of the remaining opposition to the new government, and in particular to bring the two non-ratifying states into the Union. As the first session closed, at least two House clerks and one Senate clerk were quickly put to work creating copies (originals) for transmittal. Each individual clerk had a somewhat different handwriting style, and they seem to have even consciously worked to make each state's copy unique, particularly by varying the look of the introductory paragraph to the proposed amendments.

Meanwhile, William Jackson, a member of what was known as Washington's official family, the group of aides that surrounded him performing duties as advisers, bodyguards, agents, clerks, and confidants—an early iteration of today's White House staff—was given the task of writing out thirteen identical letters for the president's signature. Our decades-long and nationwide search for documents related to the history of the First Federal Congress, accomplished in cooperation with the Ratification of the Constitution Project, turned up the originals of eight of Washington's transmittal letters. We located the letters to the governors of Massachusetts, Rhode Island, South Carolina, and very fortuitously, North Carolina, right where they should have been—that is, in those states' archives. Of course letters with George Washington's signature on them, particularly a letter transmitting the proposed amendments to the Constitution, are ideal targets for document thieves. Thus, it is no surprise that at least four of the letters have been "alienated" from their original locations. The letters to Virginia governor Beverly Randolph and Pennsylvania governor Thomas Mifflin are in the collections of the Historical Society of Pennsylvania, the first in the Dreer Collection and the second in the Gratz Collection. Oddly, the letter believed to be to New Hampshire president John Sullivan ended up in an autograph collection at the Minneapolis Public Library. Connecticut governor Samuel Huntington's letter was owned by document collector Bernard Schwartz in the 1950s, but by 1989 it was located in the Forbes Magazine Collection, collected by Malcolm Forbes in New York City. That collection has since been sold. The Papers of George Washington Project has in its files a copy from the Maryland Historical Society of a letter to an unknown governor; perhaps this is the letter to Maryland governor John Eager Howard.

We do not know for sure what method of conveyance Washington chose for his letters and their large (twenty-six-by-thirty inches) enclosures. Because there is evidence that some states' copies have not been folded, we assume that the letter and enclosure were rolled together and placed in a tubular container, probably made of leather. The absence of either postmarks or franks on the extant letters makes it likely that the president did not convey the documents through the existing postal system but instead chose to send them by messengers. He could also have entrusted them to representatives or senators who were returning home after their long and productive first session.

With the transmittal of the amendments to the states, the ratification process could begin. As was the case with the Constitution, the process moved quickly at first, but then it began to slow. New Jersey was the first to ratify on November 20, 1789, followed in relatively rapid succession by Maryland, North Carolina (which had finally ratified the Constitution in December 1789), South Carolina, New Hampshire, Delaware, New York, and Pennsylvania.

A three-month pause in the process occurred at this point, and then the much-desired ratification of both the Constitution and eleven of the twelve proposed amendments by the very independent and ornery state of Rhode Island occurred on June 11, 1790. That state's ratification document included a statement enjoining individuals elected as representatives and senators to work for a list of amendments that would have limited powers of the federal government. Though the amendments still lacked approval by two of the eleven states necessary for ratification, the political goal of bringing North Carolina and Rhode Island into the Union had been achieved.

A year and a half elapsed before Virginia, the state most responsible for their existence, finally ratified the twelve proposed amendments, and, after Thomas Jefferson's certification, all but the first two of the proposed amendments had achieved the positive vote of eleven states necessary for them to become part of the U.S. Constitution. Interestingly, three of the original states—Massachusetts, Connecticut, and Georgia—did not ratify the Bill of Rights until 1939, the 150th anniversary of the passage of these amendments by the First Federal Congress.

Virginia's road to ratification was a rough one. Its Anti-Federalist senators, Richard Henry Lee and William Grayson, brashly began that state's battle over the amendments on the same day that Congress directed Washington to send them out to the states. In a letter to the Speaker of the House of Delegates enclosing a copy of the amendments, they assured him that "nothing on our part has been omitted to procure the success of those Radical Amendments proposed by the Convention and approved by the Legislature of our Country (in this case Virginia), which as our constituent, we shall always deem it our duty with respect and reverence to obey." They continued by expressing their dissatisfaction with the proposed amendments and apprehensions about civil liberties when people are "subject to an undivided government and inhabiting a Territory so extensive as that of the United States." They announced their continued commitment to "such amendments therefore as may secure against the annihilation of the State Government." In a similar, but shorter, letter to Gov. Beverly Randolph, the senators attested to their "grief that we now send forward propositions inadequate to the purpose of real and substantial Amendments."

The critical tone of these communications conflicted with the general satisfaction on the part of most Virginia leaders in the civil rights protections contained in the proposed amendments. The General Assembly refused to publish the letters, but they were eventually leaked to the *Virginia Gazette and Public Advertiser* on December 10, 1789, and subsequently reprinted around the nation. Lee and Grayson were not the only Virginians in the First Federal Congress to decry the weakness of the amendments. Rep. Thomas Tudor Tucker wrote St. George Tucker: "You will find our Amendments to the Constitution calculated merely to amuse, rather than deceive." But in the end it was Virginia, the home of George Mason, whose language in the Virginia Declaration of Rights of 1776 so influenced the Bill of Rights; of James Madison, whose persistence in Congress resulted in the adoption of the amendments soon known as the Bill of Rights; and of Thomas Jefferson, whose forward-looking perspective recognized that the true importance of a bill if rights was the "legal check which it puts in the hands of the judiciary."

So what happened to those thirteen originals of the proposed amendments so carefully handwritten by the clerks that today have tremendous intrinsic value? In 2003 only seven of the original thirteen states—New Hampshire, Massachusetts, Connecticut, Rhode Island, New Jersey, Virginia, and South Carolina—could still claim ownership of their copies of the Bill of Rights. Here is what we know about the other six copies:

In a move much regretted by later state archivists, Delaware's ratification was noted on the bottom of its copy, which was then returned to the federal government. Thus, until recently, the National Archives had two of the originals. Delaware's copy was stored away and not exhibited and thus is in excellent condition, far better than the federal government's copy of the Bill of Rights on display in the *Charters of Freedom* exhibit in the rotunda of the National Archives. Within the past few years, Delaware's state archivist initiated negotiations with the National Archives, and I believe that the "first state's" copy is now on display in Dover.

As is all too common in times of conflict, the Civil War took its toll on manuscript collections, though those losses look miniscule next to the human losses and suffering. North Carolina's copy was stolen by a Union soldier during the war; Georgia almost certainly lost her copy when General Sherman burned Atlanta.

During a period in the late nineteenth century, Pennsylvania's public records were subjected to large-scale thefts by an individual who carried carpetbags full of documents to New York City and sold them to manuscript dealers. One of those bags probably contained the Pennsylvania copy of this precious document.

On March 29, 1911, a disastrous fire destroyed the top floors of New York's Capitol building where the state library was housed. Although some of the most important documents were rescued from a safe on the first floor, New York's copy of the Bill of Rights is not mentioned as having been saved, and it seems likely that it went up in flames or was too smoke and water damaged to save. Sometime during a 1930s renovation of the Maryland State House, that state's framed copy of the Bill of Rights, which had been displayed in one of the legislative chambers, disappeared.

Assuming that the Georgia and New York copies were lost in fires, all three of the "alienated" copies have resurfaced. One was part of an 1896 gift to the New York Public Library of more than 10,800 important manuscripts collected by Dr. Thomas Addis Emmet over the course of fifty years. The Library of Congress Manuscript Division was presented with the other by Hollywood producer/director Bernie Balaban in the 1940s. The North Carolina copy is finally back home. Others will provide most of the details of the travels of, negotiations over, and legal actions and trials concerning this document. I'll fast forward from the Civil War-era theft to the late 1990s and focus upon the role that the editors at the First Federal Congress Project played in the return of this document to North Carolina.

In the late 1990s, Washington lawyer John L. Richardson contacted my coeditor, Kenneth Bowling, seeking an opinion on the authenticity of a document. Photographs were brought to our office, but, though we told him that they could be pictures of an original Bill of Rights, we stated that we would have to see the actual document to draw any conclusions. At the time, we knew that five states were missing their originals of the amendments sent to the states by Congress but had not done much further investigation. We knew little about the previous history of the North Carolina document.

Then in 2000 Richardson again made contact, this time with a request to bring a document to our office. In the interim, we had done some research about the locations of the thirteen state copies of the Bill of Rights. We knew that if the document was an authentic "original," it was almost certain that the three candidates for ownership of this document were North Carolina, Pennsylvania, and Maryland. At the time, we had not sought information from the accession records for the copies that are in the New York Public Library and the Library of Congress.

At the appointed time, three men and a woman arrived at our office with a large box similar to one in which you would carry a work of art. Though we introduced ourselves, no introductions were forthcoming from the members of the group. When the document, surrounded by an old, chipped, ornate frame painted with gold leaf, was pulled out of the box, the four First Federal Congress Project editors and a graduate student who were present were all a bit stunned. We had little doubt that there, lying on our conference table, was an original of one of this country's founding documents. But we tried to react calmly and to find out more about the provenance of this document. Our visitors, two of whom never spoke and kept a constant eye on our every move, were completely unforthcoming. My colleagues soon became so frustrated with their behavior that they left the room.

Since it was clear that we would find out nothing from Richardson and company, I told them that it was very likely that we were looking at one of the fourteen originals of the Bill of Rights but that other experts would have to make a complete study of the document, including examining the material on which it was written, to officially authenticate the document. Six states were missing their copies, but one of those copies was in the National Archives, and it was likely, though not positively established, that two of the other five had burned in fires. Therefore, the document, if it was authentic, probably belonged to one of three states whose copies had been "alienated," the archival term for the state of being missing from its proper location—one might also say stolen. It had incredible intrinsic and monetary value, but was also potentially valueless, because under federal law the state that could prove that it had once possessed it could lay claim to it. Unaware that they already knew that the document was North Carolina's, I advised them to try to determine what state it belonged to by having a highly skilled conservator take it out of the frame and remove it from the backing on which it seemed to be mounted. I held out the possibility that there might be eighteenth-century evidence, in the form of docketing on the back of the document, which would reveal ownership.

After asking a few more questions, the entourage departed, leaving us in shock and no more enlightened about their identities or connection to the document than we had been before the encounter. I immediately called the state archivist of Maryland, Ed Papenfuse, to inquire as to whether that state's copy was framed and about the circumstances of its loss. When he reported that the ornately framed copy disappeared in the 1930s, I told him that we might have just seen Maryland's Bill of Rights, and we agreed that if another contact were made, he would come to our office for the meeting.

For almost three years, this tale of the mysterious visitors served as a great story to tell students in my documentary editing class or as part of a long answer to the standard Washington cocktail party question of "what do you do?" Then in early 2003 Ken Bowling was contacted by a friend at the Library Company of Philadelphia with a request to authenticate a copy of the Bill of Rights that the new National Constitution Center, then under construction in Philadelphia, was considering purchasing. Ken quickly agreed and began to do additional research concerning the missing copies. All of us thought that there was an excellent chance that the document would be the same one that we had seen in 2000. A notebook that contained a treasure trove of documentation, including an 8½-by-11 inch photograph of the Bill of Rights that was for sale, a photo of the reverse side of that document, and copies of 1789 dockets of documents sent to the governors of the five states that were missing their copies, soon arrived in our office. A report in the notebook reviewed the history of the copies of the Bill of Rights and the evidence gathered and concluded that the ownership of the document in question could not be determined.

As Ken and I were scanning the report, our colleague and project handwriting expert, Helen Veit, exclaimed, "You can too tell who it belongs to—it belongs to North Carolina." We all quickly agreed with Helen's assessment—the characteristic handwriting similarities between the docketing on the Bill of Rights and that on George Washington's transmittal letter to North Carolina governor Samuel Johnston were unmistakable. There was little doubt that the same clerk had written both dockets. As further evidence, the contemporary dockets from New York, Pennsylvania, Maryland, and Georgia did not match up at all with that on the back of the Bill of Rights. Within moments Ken was on the phone to report our conclusion. Not long thereafter, New York manuscript dealer Seth Kaller called and asked, "How did you do that so fast?" But when the similarities between the two dockets were pointed out, he immediately agreed with our conclusions. Thus, the potential purchasers and the agent for the sellers now found themselves negotiating from significantly altered positions. I'll just close with the comment that after we received a phone call on that March day in 2003 letting us know that a successful sting had occurred, we reacted with enthusiastic cheers and a real sense of satisfaction.

SUGGESTED READINGS

Bowling, Kenneth R. " 'A Tub to the Whale': The Founding Fathers and Adoption of the Federal Bill of Rights." *Journal of the Early Republic* 8 (1988): 223-251.

Conley, Patrick T., and John P. Kaminski, eds. *The Bill of Rights and the States: The Colonial and Revolutionary Origins of American Liberties*. Madison, Wis.: Madison House, 1992.

Veit, Helen E., Kenneth R. Bowling, and Charlene Bangs Bickford, eds. *Creating the Bill of Rights: The Documentary Record from the First Federal Congress*. Baltimore: Johns Hopkins University Press, 1991.

THE ODYSSEY OF NORTH CAROLINA'S ORIGINAL COPY OF THE BILL OF RIGHTS AND THE STATE'S CASE FOR ITS OWNERSHIP

By W. Dale Talbert and Karen A. Blum

EDITOR'S NOTE: W. Dale Talbert serves as a special deputy attorney general in the Special Litigation Section of the Attorney General's Office, where he represents state agencies, officers, and employees in significant and complex civil litigation, primarily involving constitutional issues or potentially large monetary liability. Talbert was born in Concord, North Carolina, and reared in nearby Mooresville. He graduated from the University of North Carolina at Chapel Hill in 1971, receiving bachelor degrees in English literature and speech communications. He obtained his J.D. degree from the University of North Carolina School of Law in 1974. After being licensed by the State Bar, Talbert served a tour of duty as an officer in the Air Force Judge Advocate General's Corps, stationed at Pope Air Force Base. Upon release from active duty, he was appointed as an assistant district attorney for Cumberland County and subsequently an assistant attorney general for the North Carolina Attorney General's Office. Talbert's first assignment was with the Crime Control and Public Safety Section. He subsequently was assigned to the Special Litigation Section, the Correction Section (where he served as the supervising attorney), and as special projects attorney for the Criminal Division. He returned to the Special Litigation Section in 2006. During his thirty-year career as a Department of Justice attorney, Talbert has specialized in litigating issues involving interpretation of the state's public records law and the proper application of state and federal forfeiture laws. It was his expertise in these areas of the law and his litigation experience that led to him being assigned to the team of attorneys charged with returning the Bill of Rights to the people of North Carolina.

Karen A. Blum serves as an assistant attorney general in the Services to State Agencies Section of the Attorney General's Office, where she has represented the Department of Cultural Resources since May 2005. Blum grew up in Camp Lejeune, North Carolina. She earned a degree in Japanese studies from the University of North Carolina at Chapel Hill in 1989, in the course of which she spent her junior year abroad at Nanzan University in Nagoya, Japan. She received a master's degree in Japanese studies from the University of Michigan at Ann Arbor in 1992. After four and a half years in manufacturing, Blum entered North Carolina Central University School of Law in Durham. She graduated in 2001 and served as a judicial law clerk for sixteen months at the North Carolina Court of Appeals before joining the North Carolina Attorney General's Office in November 2002. While representing the Department of Agriculture and Consumer Services, Blum was assigned to work on the Bill of Rights cases in the spring of 2003 because of her research skills and tenacity. In addition to the Bill of Rights, Blum has helped to recover several other alienated public records, including the April 18, 1777, message from the House of Commons to the senate nominating governor, secretary of state, and Council of State; the January 7, 1861, proposed resolution calling for a convention to consider secession; a May 23, 1861, letter from Jefferson Davis to the governor regarding machinery for armaments; and the battle flag of the Eighteenth North Carolina Regiment, which was captured at Petersburg, Virginia, on April 2, 1865, returned to the State by the U.S. War Department in 1905, and subsequently stolen from the North Carolina Museum of History.

AUTHORS' NOTE: Our contribution to the Bill of Rights tour was a narrated PowerPoint presentation, first given at the North Carolina Museum of History in Raleigh on September 17, 2007, of the historical facts and legal theories establishing the State's ownership of the document. In essence, the presentation was a summary preview of the evidence the State had marshaled and later would present to the Wake County Superior Court in support of a lawsuit requesting the court to declare that the State had superior legal title to the Bill of Rights to the exclusion of all others. The State lawsuit was initiated in December 2003 in response to numerous legal actions that had been filed in other state and federal courts by Robert Vires Matthews, who claimed that he had an ownership interest in the State's copy of the Bill of Rights based on an alleged contribution he made to the purchase price.

The presentation was structured around many of the documents, photographs, and expected testimony of witnesses who would have been called at trial, but it was not scripted or recorded because of ongoing federal and state litigation. For this reason, we were not able to provide a scholarly paper for this publication, as have most of the other contributors. What follows is, rather, an edited version of the State's memorandum of law that was filed with exhibits in the Wake County Superior Court in support of the State's claim that it was the sole *legal* owner of the Bill of Rights. We recognize that the edited filing does not favorably compare with the scholarly papers presented by other contributors to this publication, and that, at times, the reader may find the submission tedious, repetitious, and possibly even confusing. For this, we apologize. Our goal, however, was to present to the court every scintilla of circumstantial and direct evidence that supported the State's claim of legal *ownership* in the Bill of Rights.

As an aid to the reader, we offer the following brief explanation of the historical facts and legal theory upon which the State's claim of ownership in the Bill of Rights was based, the case law precedent that would control the court's decision, and the anticipated defenses to the State's claim. In March 2003, when the State learned that its copy of the Bill of Rights was in private hands, it was possessed by Wayne Pratt, a Connecticut antiques dealer. Pratt had purchased the manuscript from the grand-daughters of Charles A. Shotwell. The State found credible the historical evidence that the Bill of Rights was taken from the Capitol by a Union soldier from Ohio during the occupation of Raleigh in 1865, and that the soldier later sold the manuscript to Charles Shotwell, who was one of his boyhood friends.

The State's claim to legal ownership of the Bill of Rights was based upon the principle of law that private individuals cannot acquire or pass title to public records other than by act of the legislature. The State's appellate courts previously had decided in other cases that to invoke this principle of law and replevy a public record the State is required to prove three things: (1) the document in question is authentic, (2) the document is required by law to be permanently retained as a public record, (3) the document was stolen or otherwise improperly removed from a public archive. The State also is required to overcome the presumption that state officials did not lawfully relinquish possession of the document. The defendants in the lawsuit opposed the State's claim by alleging that the manuscript in question could not be proven to be the copy of the Bill of Rights sent to and received by North Carolina and, even if those facts could be proven, that the Union soldier who initially took the manuscript obtained legal title to it under the Law of War and legal theory of abandonment. The edited memorandum of law presented here presents all the circumstantial and direct evidence available to establish the elements of the State's claim of ownership in the Bill of Rights and to counter the defendants' contentions that they had obtained good title to the manuscript.

THE ODYSSEY OF THE BILL OF RIGHTS

Creation, Transmittal, and Ratification

Article VII of the United States Constitution states: "The Ratification of the Conventions of nine States, shall be sufficient for the Establishment of this Constitution between the States so ratifying the Same." On June 21, 1788, the United States Constitution became effective when New Hampshire became the ninth state to approve its ratification. North Carolina, however, declined to ratify the Constitution during its first Constitutional Convention in Hillsborough because it did not preserve certain individual rights. On August 1, 1788, the convention resolved that

> a Declaration of Rights, asserting and securing from encroachment the great principles of civil and religious liberty, and the unalienable rights of the people, together with amendments to the most ambiguous and exceptionable parts of the said Constitution of government, ought to be laid before Congress, and the Convention of the states that shall or may be called for the purpose of amending the said Constitution, for their consideration, previous to the ratification of the Constitution aforesaid on the part of the state of North-Carolina.[1]

In September 1789, the First Federal Congress proposed twelve amendments to the Constitution to be considered by the states at their respective constitutional conventions. The first proposed amendment never was adopted.[2] The second proposal was ratified in 1992 as the Twenty-seventh Amendment.[3] The remaining ten amendments, upon ratification by the states in 1791, are commonly referred to as the Bill of Rights.

In September 1789, Congress also resolved "that the President of the United States be requested to transmit to the Executives of the several States which have ratified the Constitution, Copies of the Amendments proposed by Congress, to be added thereto, and like copies to the Executives of the States of Rhode Island, and North Carolina." Congressional clerks made fourteen handwritten copies of the proposed amendments, one for each of the state executives and one for the federal government. In compliance with the congressional resolution, President George Washington transmitted handwritten copies of the proposed amendments

---

[1] *Proceedings and Debates of the Convention of North-Carolina* (Edenton: Hodge and Wills, 1789), 270-271.

[2] The rejected proposal read: "After the first enumeration required by the first Article of the Constitution, there shall be one Representative for every thirty thousand, until the number shall amount to one hundred, after which, the proportion shall be so regulated by Congress, that there shall be not less than one hundred Representatives, nor less than one Representative for every forty thousand persons, until the number of Representatives shall amount to two hundred, after which the proportion shall be so regulated by Congress, that there shall not be less than two hundred Representatives, nor more than one Representative for every fifty thousand persons."

[3] "No law, varying the compensation for the services of the Senators and Representatives, shall take effect, until an election of Representatives shall have intervened." U.S. Constitution, amend. 27.

United States October 2nd 1789.

Sir,

In pursuance of the enclosed resolution I have the honor to transmit to your Excellency a copy of the amendments proposed to be added to the Constitution of the United States.

I have the honor to be,
with due consideration,
Your Excellency's
most obedient servant.

G Washington

His Excellency
Samuel Johnston.

George Washington's letter of October 2, 1789, transmitting North Carolina's original copy of the proposed bill of rights to Gov. Samuel Johnston. Image courtesy of the State Archives, N.C. Office of Archives and History, Raleigh.

to the executives of Delaware, Pennsylvania, New Jersey, Georgia, Connecticut, Massachusetts, Maryland, South Carolina, New Hampshire, Virginia, and New York—the eleven states that had ratified the Constitution—and to the executives of Rhode Island and North Carolina, which had not yet ratified. An original copy was also kept by the federal government in New York.

On October 2, 1789, President Washington sent a letter to North Carolina governor Samuel Johnston transmitting a copy of the resolves of Congress and the proposed amendments for North Carolina's consideration. Governor Johnston forwarded President Washington's letter, the manuscript resolves of Congress, and the manuscript Bill of Rights to the House of Commons at the 1789-1790 session of the General Assembly for consideration. These dispatches from the president initially were received by the House of Commons, but both houses considered and approved the proposed amendments. North Carolina ratified the United States Constitution on November 21, 1789, at a second constitutional convention, resolving that "this convention, in behalf of the freemen, citizens and inhabitants of the state of North-Carolina, do adopt and ratify the said constitution and form of government."[4]

On December 22, 1789, the General Assembly also ratified all twelve proposed amendments to the United States Constitution:

> BE it therefore enacted by the General Assembly of the State of North-Carolina, and it is hereby enacted by the Authority of the same, That the said Amendments, agreeable to the fifth Article of the original Constitution, be held and ratified on the Part of this State, as Articles in Addition to and Amendments of the Constitution of the United States of *America*.[5]

On January 8, 1790, President Washington addressed both houses of Congress, stating:

> I embrace with great satisfaction the opportunity which now presents itself of congratulating you on the present favorable prospects of our public affairs. The recent accession of the important State of North Carolina to the constitution of the United States, (of which official information has been received;) the rising credit and respectability of our country; the general and increasing good-will towards the Government of the Union; and the concord, peace, and plenty with which we are blessed, are circumstances auspicious in an eminent degree to our national prosperity.[6]

On May 25, 1790, North Carolina governor Alexander Martin transmitted to President Washington "an Act of the General Assembly of the State passed at this last Session entitled 'An Act to ratify the Amendments to the Constitution of the

---

[4] Francois-Xavier Martin, comp., *The Public Acts of the General Assembly of North Carolina* (New Bern: Martin and Ogden, 1804), 460-465.

[5] James Iredell, comp., *Laws of the State of North-Carolina* (Edenton: Hodge and Wills, 1791), 672-673.

[6] Joseph Gales Sr., comp., *Annals of Congress* (Washington: Gales and Seaton, 1834), 1:969-971.

United States.' "[7] On June 11, 1790, President Washington presented to the United States Senate and House of Representatives an excerpt from Governor Martin's letter and an enrolled copy of the North Carolina General Assembly's act to ratify the amendments.[8]

Retention as a Public Record

The State of North Carolina has stored and permanently retained its public records, including legislative records, since the beginning of its colonial period (1663-1776), with some currently held legislative records dating back to the 1708 session of the assembly. During the revolutionary period (1776-1783) and federal period (1783-1815), before the assembly had a permanent seat of government, State House, or Capitol building in which to meet, the assemblies' principal clerks had the duty to permanently preserve the records of all previous assemblies and provincial conventions and transport the archival records from meeting place to meeting place. When the assembly was not in session, the principal clerks stored the legislative records in their homes or private offices. During the federal period, the secretary of state was expected to have preserved even the colonial legislative acts that had subsequently been repealed or disallowed by the British Crown. Legislative records, including ratified bills and attendant papers, were folded, endorsed, and bundled for filing by legislative clerks. The bundled records were placed in the custody of the assemblies' principal clerks for permanent storage. President Washington's letter, the 1789 resolves of Congress, and the Bill of Rights were legislative records of the House of Commons that would have been folded, endorsed, bundled, and stored with the archival legislative records.

In 1788, a state convention selected Raleigh as the permanent seat of government. In December 1793, the assembly directed that as soon as the State House then being constructed on Union Square was completed, the assembly and all public officers of the state, including the secretary of state, were to move into the building "with all the public papers and Records of their Several offices."[9] The assembly and the state officers moved into the State House when it was finished in 1796. The public papers and records of state government, including those of the assembly and the secretary of state, were retained and preserved in the State House and in two adjacent "fireproof" buildings until the State House burned in 1831.

Rather than letting the state's archival records be consumed by the fire, state officers and employees working in the State House and many citizens retrieved them from the burning building, likely in recognition of the importance of the documents. Nearly all of the state's public records, except for some holdings of the State Library, were saved. The records were in disarray, however, from the

---

[7] See *Journal of the Second Session of the Senate of the United States of America* (Washington: Gales and Seaton, 1820), 154-155.

[8] Gales, *Annals of Congress*, 1:1024, 2:1693.

[9] House resolution, December 26, 1793, General Assembly Session Records, 1793-1794, Box 1, North Carolina State Archives.

process of hurriedly bringing them out of the burning State House. By legislative resolution of December 1831, the records were placed in the temporary custody of the governor, who was requested to have them arranged in proper order and then returned to the appropriate state-officer custodians. The governor complied with the resolution and informed the assembly in November 1832 that he had delivered the sorted and properly arranged legislative archival records to the secretary of state, because he had no room in his residence, the Government House, and sought the assembly's consent for that disposition.

A new state government office building, the Capitol, was constructed on the same site as the former State House and was occupied in 1840. All official documents and public records of the executive, legislative, and judicial branches of government, including all archival records of previous assemblies, were moved to and stored in the new Capitol. The manuscript Bill of Rights, being an archival record of the assembly required to be permanently retained and preserved, would have been stored in the Capitol with the assembly's archival biennial session records. Although it cannot be determined with certainty where in the Capitol the manuscript Bill of Rights was stored, it would have been kept with other archival legislative records that are known to have been in various places, including the primary legislative archives storage room on the third floor outside the senate gallery and in the secretary of state's office on the first floor. Some archival legislative records were stored on shelves and cabinets in the state geologist's office and in the State Library, both of which were on the third floor. The Bill of Rights remained in the possession of the State—preserved in the Capitol—until it was taken by a Union soldier from Ohio during the occupation of Raleigh in 1865.

The Theft

Gen. William Tecumseh Sherman's Union troops crossed into North Carolina in early March 1865. On April 12, as Sherman approached Raleigh, a train departed the city carrying the state papers and records necessary for continued operation of the government and prosecution of the war, funds of the treasury and banks, and state officials who had evacuated the capital. Bvt. Maj. Gen. Judson Kilpatrick, who commanded the Union Third Cavalry Division, reached Raleigh in the early hours of April 13. Confederate general Joseph Wheeler, Gov. Zebulon B. Vance, and the last of the Confederate troops had left Raleigh the night before.[10]

After accepting the surrender of Raleigh, Kilpatrick continued his pursuit of Wheeler. The Fifth Ohio Cavalry, commanded by Maj. George H. Rader, was left behind to protect the town until Brig. Gen. Harrison C. Hobart's brigade of the Fourteenth Army Corps arrived.[11] The troopers were followed very shortly by the

[10] *The War of the Rebellion: A Compilation of the Official Records of the Union and Confederate Armies,* 150 vols. (Washington: Government Printing Office, 1880-1901), ser. 1, 47, pt. 1:712, 937.
[11] *Raleigh Daily Standard,* April 17, 1865.

Ninety-fourth Ohio Volunteer Infantry, organized at Camp Piqua, near Troy, Ohio. Tens of thousands more Union soldiers streamed into Raleigh during the day and established camps wherever open space could be found: on Union Square; in the four parks surrounding the Capitol; on the lawns of private residences; and on the grounds of the State Insane Asylum, later known as Dorothea Dix Hospital. Sherman arrived in Raleigh later on April 13 and established headquarters in the governor's mansion (or Government House) six blocks south of the Capitol on Fayetteville Street.

Most of Sherman's 100,000-man army, containing many regiments from Ohio, camped in or near Raleigh. At the time, the city was approximately ten blocks square, with Union Square in the center. The Fourteenth Army Corps, containing approximately sixteen Ohio regiments, was camped inside the city limits at its northern and western fringes. Portions of the Twentieth Army Corps, containing approximately eight Ohio regiments, were camped at the State Insane Asylum, while others bivouacked at the southwestern edge of Raleigh or east of the city limits. The Twenty-third Army Corps, which included many Ohio regiments, was also camped just east of the city. The Fifteenth Army Corps and Seventeenth Army Corps, also containing many regiments of Ohio troops, encamped, respectively, at St. Mary's Hospital near the intersection of Hillsboro and St. Mary's streets, and within a few miles of Raleigh.

During the occupation of Raleigh, Union soldiers were allowed to leave their regiments' places of encampment when not performing military duties. Many did so and visited the city's sights and entered its buildings, including the Capitol. Many other Union soldiers went into the Capitol to perform military assignments, particularly work details related to crating and removing Confederate supplies and other property stored there. Union soldiers attended meetings held in the Capitol, specifically in the legislative chambers, for official and social purposes, or went into the Capitol to conduct business with the provost marshal for Raleigh, whose office was established on April 13 in the governor's two-room suite on the first floor. All of the Union soldiers who went into the Capitol had unfettered access to the House and senate chambers, the State Library, the state geologist's office, and the rooms adjacent to the senate and House galleries, including the legislative archives storage room at the entrance to the senate gallery. Soldiers also had access to the unoccupied offices of former state officials, including those of the treasurer and the secretary of state, until replacements were appointed by the Union government and the offices reoccupied.

During the Georgia and Carolinas campaigns, General Sherman's army earned a well-deserved reputation for destruction and seizure of property owned by the Confederate states and private persons and for the lack of discipline among the troops, especially Sherman's "Bummers." "Bummers" was a nickname applied to foragers of Sherman's army who were authorized to gather, from any available source, rations and supplies of any sort and quantity useful to their commands. The practice of taking Confederate state government and privately owned property was not limited to the Bummers. Other soldiers in Sherman's army, both officers and enlisted men, took documents and public papers owned by the

Confederate states as "trophies" or souvenirs of their military service from the cities they passed through or occupied.

On the day that Raleigh surrendered, a United States Army Signal Corps station was established atop the Capitol's dome to relay signals from General Sherman's headquarters to troops encamped around the city. Signal Corps members had free access to all areas in the Capitol. Some Signal Corps soldiers even scribbled graffiti in the rafters of the attic over the senate chamber.

Almost immediately after the Capitol's occupation, Union troops were assigned to take down and package dozens of captured Union battle flags that had been suspended from the galleries above the House and senate chambers. Troops were also detailed to dismantle, crate for shipping, and remove from the Capitol numerous lighthouse lenses and their operating mechanisms that were stored on and around the rotunda gallery.

On April 14, a meeting of Union soldiers was held in the treasurer's office to form the Society of the Army of the Tennessee. The Army of the Tennessee had a large presence in Raleigh at the time, and many of its regiments were from Ohio. When the 117th Regiment of New York Volunteers arrived on April 14, its regimental surgeon reported that the contents of the Capitol were in disarray:

> The interior of the capitol, presented a scene of the utmost confusion. Bound legislative documents, and maps, lay strewn about the floor of the library. The museum rooms were in even a worse plight. The sash and glass of the cases had been broken, and many of the specimens of natural history had been "confiscated." The geological collections had been wantonly broken and promiscuously scattered.[12]

A captain in the Seventy-sixth Ohio Volunteer Infantry wrote his wife from Raleigh on April 14 that he had visited the Capitol and had taken a legislative bill regarding peace commissioners being sent from each of the southern states, pamphlets regarding contracts for the State Capitol, and a 1792 bill concerning improvement of the navigation of the New River.[13]

The *Philadelphia Inquirer* reported that by April 16, the state's archives had been picked through by "curious hands": "The room in which the archives of the State are kept is but very little disturbed. From floor to ceiling the superscriptions of the documents may be read; ranged in regular order. Curious hands have been busy with the Secession records, and many of them strew the floor."[14] Many other records, including all of the state treasurer's reports, were taken during the occupation of the Capitol.

On April 19, a meeting open to all Union troops from Ohio was held in the Capitol's senate chamber. The purpose of the meeting was to select from

[12] James A. Mowris, *A History of the One Hundred and Seventeenth Regiment, New York Volunteers* (1866; reprint, with a foreword by Edwin C. Bearrs, Hamilton, N.Y.: Edmonston Publishing, 1996), 210.

[13] John J. Metzgar to Carrie Metzgar, April 14, 1865, John J. Metzgar Papers, #4939, Southern Historical Collection, Wilson Library, University of North Carolina at Chapel Hill.

[14] *Philadelphia Inquirer*, April 26, 1865.

among the Ohio troops in General Sherman's army delegates to represent the army members at an Ohio state convention that would nominate candidates for governor and other state offices. Given the importance of this meeting, it is likely that a substantial number of soldiers from Ohio attended.

There are many other documented accounts of Union soldiers taking public records from the state's archives in the early days of the occupation of Raleigh. A January 7, 1861, proposed resolution of the North Carolina General Assembly calling for a complete protection of rights under the Constitution was taken. It was returned to the State Archives on June 29, 1968, by Southern Illinois University in Carbondale, Illinois. The reverse of the manuscript bears an endorsement with the following notation handwritten below: "Taken from the Records of the State, at Raleigh N.C. April 15, 1865 By Capt. S. B. Wheelock A.A.A.G 3d Brig. 2 Div. 20 AC." Capt. Samuel B. Wheelock served as the acting assistant adjutant general of the Third Brigade, Second Division, Twentieth Army Corps, which occupied Raleigh in April 1865.[15] Another January 7, 1861, proposed resolution of the North Carolina General Assembly calling for a convention of the state to consider secession was also taken. It too was returned to the State Archives on November 28, 2006, by a historic manuscripts dealer in Beverly Hills, California. The reverse of the manuscript bears an endorsement with the following notation handwritten below: "Taken from the Hall of Records, Raleigh N.C. on the 15th day of April 1865 By Capt. S. B. Wheelock A.A.A.G 3d Brig. 2 Div. 20 AC."[16]

Several senate records created on the same day have been permanently retained in the North Carolina State Archives. A January 7, 1861, proposed resolution of the General Assembly regarding taking possession of United States forts in North Carolina is preserved in the State Archives. The endorsement on the reverse of the manuscript states that the resolution was read and laid upon the table. This proposed resolution was maintained in and among the records of the General Assembly in the State Capitol until being transferred to the custody of the North Carolina Historical Commission, now the Office of Archives and History, on March 18, 1915.[17]

[15] Second Amended State's Memorandum of Law in Support of its Motion for Summary Judgment, *N.C. Att'y Gen. Roy Cooper ex rel. State v. N.C.'s Original Copy of the Bill of Rights*, No. 03-CVS-16816 (Wake County Superior Court, March 20, 2008), Exhibit 125 (affidavit of Jesse R. Lankford Jr. re. removed documents). A copy of the recovered document is in General Assembly Session Records, 1860-1861, Box 6, Miscellaneous Senate Resolutions; the original is in the Vault Collection, V.C. 33, North Carolina State Archives.

[16] Second Amended State's Memorandum of Law, Exhibit 125 (affidavit of Jesse R. Lankford Jr. re. removed documents). A copy of the recovered document is in General Assembly Session Records, 1860-1861, Box 6, Miscellaneous Senate Resolutions; the original is in the Vault Collection, V.C. 33, North Carolina State Archives.

[17] Senate resolution, January 7, 1861, copy in General Assembly Session Records, 1860-1861, Box 6, Miscellaneous Senate Resolutions, North Carolina State Archives; North Carolina Historical Commission, Record of Events, 1910-1919, entry for March 18, 1915, p. 32, Department of Archives and History, Director's Office, North Carolina State Archives.

An 1861 manuscript journal of the North Carolina Senate has also been permanently retained in the General Assembly Session Records of the State Archives. The journal summarizes the daily proceedings of the senate during the 1861 session. It contains a January 7, 1861, entry documenting that resolutions previously offered by Senator Thomas of Jackson were referred to the Committee on Federal Relations. The January 7, 1861, entry also documents that a resolution introduced by Senator Turner regarding taking possession of United States forts in North Carolina had been tabled.[18]

On April 29, 1865, State Treasurer Jonathan Worth informed Gov. Zebulon B. Vance by telegraph that Gen. John M. Schofield had directed Worth to deliver to Raleigh the state papers that government officials had removed during the evacuation.[19] On June 12, Lt. Col. J. A. Campbell, by command of General Schofield, issued Special Order No. 88, ordering that all archives and other property required by law to be kept in the custody of the North Carolina secretary of state be delivered to the newly appointed secretary, Charles R. Thomas. Colonel Campbell's order further directed that the secretary of state's offices in the Capitol be turned over to Thomas.[20]

During and after the occupation of Raleigh, Treasurer (later governor) Worth attempted to recover state property, which was "scattered from the mountains to the sea shore and every where smuggled." In a letter dated September 15, 1865, Worth stated in frustration:

> I failed at Washington to get the Govt. to give up the State property captured *after the proclamation by [Generals] Sherman and Schofield to the army and people of N. C. that peace existed.* This capture was rapacious and illegal, as I think, and consequently impolitic. I succeeded however in getting an order forbidding *further* captures.[21]

A portion of North Carolina's archives was found in Morrisania, New York. The *Westchester Gazette* reported in October 1865 that some of North Carolina's stolen colonial and revolutionary archives were supposed to have been sent to the secretary of war in Washington, but the officer who delivered them to the post

[18] *Journal of the Senate of the General Assembly of the State of North-Carolina at its Session of 1860-'61* (Raleigh: John Spelman, 1861), 145-146.

[19] Jonathan Worth to Zebulon B. Vance (telegram), April 29, 1865, Governors' Papers, Zebulon B. Vance, G.P. 183, North Carolina State Archives.

[20] Special Order No. 88, June 12, 1865, Governors' Papers, William W. Holden, G.P. 185, North Carolina State Archives; also transcribed in Governors' Letterbooks, William W. Holden, G.L.B. 51, p. 1, North Carolina State Archives.

[21] Jonathan Worth to S. Whitaker, September 15, 1865, in J. G. de Roulhac Hamilton, ed., *The Correspondence of Jonathan Worth*, 2 vols. (Raleigh: North Carolina Historical Commission, 1909), 1:421.

office did not have the correct postage and failed to send the package.[22] It is unclear whether all of these documents were ever recovered.[23]

In a November 7, 1868, report to the General Assembly on the status of the state's public records, Secretary of State Henry J. Menninger indicated that most of the state's archives had been recovered.[24] North Carolina's original copy of the Bill of Rights, however, was not recovered, and there is no credible evidence that its location was known by state officers until 1897.

Discovery and Attempts to Recover

According to a June 10, 1897, article in the Raleigh *News and Observer*, North Carolina's copy of the Bill of Rights was discovered to be hanging on the wall of an office in the Indianapolis Board of Trade Building in Indianapolis, Indiana. As originally reported by the *Indianapolis News* on May 10, 1897, it was described as belonging to Charles A. Shotwell, who was quoted as saying:

> I was living at Troy, O[hio], at the close of the war, thirty-two years ago. I got it off a soldier in an Ohio regiment. I believe it cost me $5. He took it from the State House at Raleigh, N.C. when that place was pillaged by Sherman's army.[25]

In response to the article, North Carolina Supreme Court justice Walter Clark wrote to North Carolina's secretary of state, Dr. Cyrus Thompson, on June 19, imploring him to make an attempt to recover the "lost record" of the state. Justice Clark further offered his opinion that the document belonged to North Carolina and could be recovered "anywhere at any time." Secretary of State Thompson agreed. In a letter to a citizen who sent him a newspaper clipping of a similar article, Thompson opined that, "[i]f the clipping is true, the parchment evidently belongs to this State, and ought to be, either in this office, or in the State Library."[26]

Secretary of State Thompson attempted to negotiate the return of the Bill of Rights through the *Indianapolis News* and Indiana secretary of state William D. Owen. At Thompson's request, Owen contacted Shotwell, who confirmed the account printed in the *Indianapolis News*. As related in a September 30, 1897, letter from Owen to Thompson, Charles Shotwell stated that the soldier who sold him the manuscript told him that "he, and others, took the document and

[22] *Raleigh Daily Sentinel*, April 16, 1866 (reprinting *Westchester Gazette* article).

[23] In 1906, however, Senator Furnifold Simmons successfully proposed joint legislation in the United States Congress requiring that certain records of the colonial and federal periods in North Carolina be transferred from the Bureau of Rolls and Library back to the State. Joint Resolution, February 15, 1906, *Congressional Record: Containing the Proceedings and Debates of the Fifty-ninth Congress, First Session* (Washington: Government Printing Office, 1906), 40, pt. 3:2606.

[24] "Report of Secretary of State," November 7, 1868, pp. 1-2 [in Executive and Legislative Documents, Session 1868-'69; title page and publication data missing].

[25] *Indianapolis News*, May 10, 1897; Raleigh *News and Observer*, June 10, 1897.

[26] Cyrus Thompson to G. W. F. Harper, September 24, 1897, Secretary of State, Correspondence, Series I, Box 184, North Carolina State Archives.

other articles from the State House at Raleigh as souvenirs of that occasion." Owen further wrote that he had personally examined the document and believed it to be genuine. He stated, however, that Shotwell would not say what his disposition to return the document might be. By letter dated October 2, 1897, Thompson thanked Owen for his efforts.[27]

On October 5, 1897, the *News and Observer* again reported that Charles A. Shotwell possessed one of the original copies of the twelve proposed amendments to the United States Constitution. The *News and Observer* printed in full a September 25, 1897, letter from Secretary of State Thompson to the *Indianapolis News* stating in part:

> I trust I may trespass so far upon your kindness as to ask you to write to me whether the facts set forth in the clipping are true, in order that I may, if possible, secure the return of the document to this Department; and I shall be very much obliged.

The *News and Observer* also reprinted the October 1, 1897, response by the *Indianapolis News* that Shotwell "certainly would not give it up on any 'demand,' no matter from whom such demand might come." The *News and Observer* also reprinted the September 30 reply from Secretary of State Owen to Secretary of State Thompson. Like state officials, the *News and Observer* concluded that the Bill of Rights was "clearly the property of North Carolina and should be in the State's archives." Nevertheless, the State failed to negotiate the return of the manuscript Bill of Rights from Shotwell in 1897.[28]

State officials heard nothing more about the manuscript until 1925. In a February 6, 1925, letter to Professor J. G. de Roulhac Hamilton at the University of North Carolina, Charles I. Reid, a New York promoter, stated that he had possession of North Carolina's original copy of the Bill of Rights, which "was taken from the state house at Raleigh by one of the Union soldiers who came from Ohio."[29]

Charles A. Shotwell had a connection to Charles I. Reid through Shotwell's son, Grier Moore Shotwell. Grier Shotwell served with Reid during World War I in the Signal Corps Photographic Unit when they were both assigned to the American Expeditionary Force North Russia. Grier Shotwell and Reid developed a close friendship that continued after the war until Reid's accidental death in 1939. A daughter of Grier Shotwell (a granddaughter of Charles A. Shotwell) found among her mother's personal and family papers shortly after her mother's death a photograph of her father wearing a military uniform and holding a box camera. Another man in the photograph is also dressed in a military uniform and holding a reel-to-reel movie camera. In the background

---

[27] Cyrus Thompson to *Indianapolis News*, September 25, 1897, William D. Owen to Cyrus Thompson, September 30, 1897, Thompson to Owen, October 2, 1897, Secretary of State, Correspondence, Series I, Boxes 184, 185, North Carolina State Archives.

[28] Raleigh *News and Observer*, October 5, 1897.

[29] Chas. I. Reid to J. D. [*sic*] De Roulhac Hamilton, February 6, 1925, Department of Archives and History, Director, General Correspondence, Box 53, North Carolina State Archives.

are buildings with "onion domes," typical features of Russian architecture. A copy of the same photograph is filed in the National Archives.[30]

Grier Shotwell's daughter also found among her mother's papers a signed carbon copy of a typewritten letter from her grandfather, Charles A. Shotwell, to Reid, dated November 22, 1924. In the letter, Shotwell stated that his son, Grier, previously had sent to Reid a "photo-print of the parchment he has in his possession," and that he is giving Reid "a history of that parchment coming into [his] hands."[31]

In response to Reid's February 6, 1925, letter, Professor Hamilton replied on February 9, advising Reid that the Bill of Rights was the property of the State of North Carolina and requesting that it be returned. After receiving Hamilton's reply, Reid wrote to a collector, Gen. Julian S. Carr of Durham, offering him "a first opportunity to obtain this most important of historical documents, for your private collection or for presentation to the state." General Carr, however, had died, and the letter was forwarded to Col. Fred A. Olds of the North Carolina Hall of History.[32]

By letter dated March 24, 1925, R. B. House, secretary of the Historical Commission (now the Office of Archives and History), informed Reid that the document had been stolen from the Capitol in 1865, and "therefore, title to it has never passed from the State of North Carolina to any individual." Secretary House further advised Reid that "no person in the State of North Carolina would be willing to purchase the document under such conditions and thus give commercial standing to such an act as its being taken under the circumstances attending its disappearance." On March 25, Reid again offered to sell the Bill of Rights to the State and advised House that the possessor was an old man who had purchased the document in 1866 from a soldier in Sherman's army who had carried it home with him to Tippecanoe, Ohio. In response to Reid's renewed attempt to market the Bill of Rights, House replied that it was clearly the property of the State of North Carolina, and "[s]o long as it remains away from the official custody of North Carolina, it will serve as a memorial of individual theft." No further written communications from Reid to state officials have been found among the state's records.[33]

---

[30] Photograph No. NWDNS-111-SC-62503; Signal Corps Photographs of American Military Activity, 1754-1954; Records of the Office of the Chief Signal Officer, 1860-1982, Record Group 111; National Archives and Records Administration, Special Media Archives Services Division (College Park).

[31] Second Amended State's Memorandum of Law, Exhibit 119 (C. A. Shotwell to Charles I. Reid, November 22, 1924).

[32] Reid to Julian S. Carr, March 16, 1925, Thomas M. Gorman to Col. Fred A. Olds, March 19, 1925, Department of Archives and History, Director, General Correspondence, Box 53, North Carolina State Archives.

[33] House to Reid, March 24, 1925, Reid to House, March 25, 1925, House to Reid, April 7, 1925, Department of Archives and History, Director, General Correspondence, Box 53, North Carolina State Archives.

In the early to mid-1990s, Charles Shotwell's granddaughters—Grier Shotwell's children—enlisted the help of an Indianapolis attorney to market and sell the copy of the Bill of Rights that they possessed. In or around June 1995, Wayne E. Pratt, an antiques dealer doing business as Wayne Pratt, Inc. (WPI) in Woodbury, Connecticut, engaged the services of Washington, D.C., attorney John L. Richardson to help him purchase and resell a "document."[34] According to the engagement letter, Richardson and his firm were to "serve as [Pratt's] counsel and legal representative to assist in the purchase and sale of a document, currently in the possession of others."[35]

In October 1995, Richardson wrote to Betty McCain, secretary of the North Carolina Department of Cultural Resources, offering to sell to the State what was clandestinely described as an "article."[36] Although there were some preliminary negotiations, the department refused to buy back the stolen Bill of Rights.

It was around this time that Robert Vires Matthews first learned of an authentic handwritten copy of the Bill of Rights in private hands. Pratt told Matthews, "from the beginning," that he and Richardson were trying to sell a copy of the Bill of Rights to the State of North Carolina.[37] Matthews, one of Pratt's longtime friends, was also one of his regular customers and an occasional business partner. Matthews is a self-described "entrepreneur," primarily involved in real estate and investments but with interests in numerous businesses involving, among other things, construction and software. Matthews's business headquarters in the mid-1990s was First New Haven Capital Corporation in New Haven, Connecticut, near Pratt's Woodbury, Connecticut, antiques store. Matthews's principal residence was in Washington Depot, Connecticut, also near Woodbury.

On September 10, 1997, WPI sent $50,000 by wire to the trust account of the Indianapolis attorney for the Shotwell granddaughters. The money was in payment for an option, in Pratt's favor, to purchase or make an initial deposit on what the parties subsequently described in the bill of sale as "one of the original manuscripts of the Bill of Rights, on vellum, with approximate dimensions of 31" x 26.5"."[38]

In late 1997 or early 1998, Dr. Kenneth R. Bowling, a senior staff member of the First Federal Congress (FFC) Project in Washington, D.C., was contacted by telephone by a person representing himself as the attorney for an individual who

---

[34] Pratt died on July 26, 2007. WPI is reportedly selling its inventory and will close permanently.

[35] Second Amended State's Memorandum of Law, Exhibit 21 (John L. Richardson to WPI, June 23, 1995).

[36] Second Amended State's Memorandum of Law, Exhibits 22-1 (John L. Richardson to Betty Ray McCain, October 24, 1995) and 23-1 (same to same, January 16, 1996). The content of the mid-October conversation referred to in the first exhibit is unknown.

[37] Second Amended State's Memorandum of Law, Exhibit 20 (deposition of Robert Vires Matthews).

[38] Second Amended State's Memorandum of Law, Exhibit 26 (bill of sale).

claimed to possess and wanted to sell an original manuscript copy of the Bill of Rights. The FFC Project is a chartered university research center affiliated with the Department of History at George Washington University. The caller did not specifically identify himself or his client. He did, however, send to Dr. Bowling photographs of the front of the manuscript that his client allegedly possessed. The caller did not contact Dr. Bowling again.

Dr. Bowling examined the photographs of the manuscript and concluded that it was highly probable that the document was an original copy of the Bill of Rights. He could not, however, positively identify the manuscript as being an authentic original copy, primarily because photographs of its reverse, where a docket might have been written, had not been provided. "Docket" refers to a summary or other brief identification of a document normally written on the manuscript itself by the recipient or, in the case of an official record, by a clerk of a government official or body. A docket usually includes the date of the document and sometimes the date it was received, answered, or entered into the records or archives of the government official or body. The term "docket sheet" refers to a docket written on a separate sheet of plain paper wrapped around a folded document, rather than on the manuscript itself. The term "endorsement," instead of "docket" or "docket sheet," is also used to describe this informational notation.

According to Matthews, Pratt invited him to become an investor in the purchase and resale of the Bill of Rights sometime after WPI obtained the option. Matthews was a self-described "passive investor" in WPI's plan to purchase and sell the Bill of Rights, and he would receive "fifty percent of the upside" if any profit were made.[39] Matthews and Pratt flew to Indiana to meet the Shotwell granddaughters' attorney and inspect the document. On June 2, 1999, Matthews signed a $150,000 check in favor of "Wayne Pratt, Inc." The check was written on the general disbursement account of First New Haven Capital Corporation, Matthews Related Entities. Matthews holds 100 percent of the shares of the First New Haven Capital Corporation. The check was deposited into the general business account of Wayne E. Pratt, Inc.

On February 23, 2000, WPI as "Buyer," the Shotwell granddaughters as "Sellers," and the granddaughters' attorney as "Escrow Agent" entered into an escrow agreement to facilitate the sale and purchase of the Bill of Rights that they possessed. The escrow agreement provided that on or before February 24, 2000, a Shotwell representative would bring the document to Washington, D.C., for authentication. A representative of WPI would then have three hours in which to purchase the Bill of Rights. If WPI elected to buy the Bill of Rights, the escrowed funds totaling $200,000 would be distributed to the Shotwell granddaughters' attorney, and the WPI representative would receive the manuscript at the authentication site in Washington, D.C.

---

[39] Second Amended State's Memorandum of Law, Exhibit 20 (deposition of Robert Vires Matthews).

The same day that WPI, the Shotwell granddaughters, and their attorney entered into the escrow agreement, WPI sent $150,000 by wire transfer to the granddaughters' attorney's trust account. The bill of sale had already been executed in counterparts by the granddaughters, as "Sellers." One Shotwell granddaughter executed the bill of sale in Georgia on January 7, 2000. On February 15, the other granddaughter executed the bill of sale in Indianapolis. "Wayne A. [sic] Pratt, Inc., a corporation" was identified as the "Buyer." "Wayne Pratt, Inc." as "Buyer" also entered into a written mutual confidentiality agreement with the Shotwell granddaughters, the "Sellers" of the document, agreeing, among other things, not to disclose information about the history of the document.

On or about February 24, 2000, the Indianapolis attorney for the Shotwell granddaughters and Richardson, on behalf of WPI, entered into a suspension agreement to suspend the sale and purchase of the Bill of Rights to allow WPI to conduct a more thorough analysis of the document. Soon thereafter, Dr. Bowling was contacted again by persons claiming to have an authentic copy of the Bill of Rights, this time in person. Sometime during the first quarter of that year, a person identifying himself as an attorney had called and arranged to have what he claimed to be an original copy of the Bill of Rights brought to the FFC Project for authentication. In approximately March 2000, five unidentified persons, one female and four males, came to the FFC Project offices in Washington, D.C. The group presented to Dr. Bowling, Charlene Bickford, the project director, and Helen Veit, another FFC Project senior researcher, a cardboard carrying case containing a manuscript framed behind a piece of glass with only its front visible.

The FFC Project scholars examined the manuscript and believed that it was highly probable that the manuscript was an authentic copy of the Bill of Rights. Their opinion was based upon examination of the handwriting, which appeared to be in one of the same formal hands as other known copies of the Bill of Rights that they had examined, and the apparent authenticity of the signatures. The possessors of the document were told, however, that it could not be determined to which state the copy of the Bill of Rights originally had been sent without inspecting the reverse of the manuscript to determine whether it bore a docket. The possessors did not offer such an inspection and left with the manuscript.

The next month, on April 20, 2000, WPI was billed for $2,500 by Paper Conservation Studios, Inc., in New York City for services described on the invoice as "remov[ing] old cardboard mount and residue" from "a [p]archment document dated 1789."[40] Several weeks after having the backing removed from the Bill of Rights, WPI decided to purchase the document, although its research into the authenticity of the document was not yet complete. In early June 2000, agents for the parties executed a mutual release, the primary purpose of which was to discharge each other from all claims that might arise from the sale and purchase of the Bill of Rights. The mutual release recognized, however, the

[40] Second Amended State's Memorandum of Law, Exhibit 32 (invoice, April 20, 2000).

existence of the parties' escrow agreement and the suspension agreement entered into on or about February 24, 2000, to permit WPI to more fully analyze the Bill of Rights. The mutual release also stated that, based upon subsequent extensive research with respect to the value of the Bill of Rights, WPI had elected to purchase the document according to the terms in the escrow and suspension agreements. On June 6, 2000, the Indianapolis attorney signed the release on behalf of the Shotwell granddaughters. On June 12, John Richardson signed for WPI.

On January 16, 2003, almost three years after purchasing the Bill of Rights, Pratt gave to art and rare document dealers Peter H. Tillou and William S. Reese a written "two-month option to sell the Bill of Rights, at a price [of] five million dollars." The same day, Pratt agreed in writing to pay Tillou and Reese "a net commission of $1 million from the sale of the Bill of Rights when sold for $5 million."[41]

Pratt continued to seek Richardson's legal services to assist WPI in selling the Bill of Rights. Apparently, by February 2003, WPI had targeted a prospective buyer. A representative of the National Constitution Center (NCC) in Philadelphia, Pennsylvania, requested Dr. Bowling to attempt to authenticate a manuscript being offered for sale to the NCC and described by the seller as one of the original handwritten copies of the Bill of Rights. The NCC representative also requested that if Dr. Bowling concluded that the manuscript was an authentic copy, he confirm the seller's claim that it was impossible to determine which state had originally received it.

To assist Dr. Bowling in his authentication process, the NCC provided photographs of the front and the docket on the reverse of the Bill of Rights, as well as photocopies of dockets or docket sheets from documents known to have been received in or around 1789 by the governors and legislatures of the states that, in 2003, did not possess their copies of the Bill of Rights—Georgia, Maryland, New York, North Carolina, and Pennsylvania. Dr. Bowling has identified one of these dockets as the one on President Washington's October 2, 1789, letter to North Carolina governor Johnston transmitting to the state one of the original handwritten copies of the Bill of Rights. The NCC also provided a photocopy of the docket on the reverse of President Washington's June 19, 1789, letter to Governor Johnston and the North Carolina Council of State.

Based upon an examination of photographs of the Bill of Rights and the docket on its reverse, and the photocopies of other dockets, Dr. Bowling and the other FFC Project scholars concluded that the manuscript offered for sale to the NCC in 2003 was one of the original handwritten copies of the Bill of Rights drafted by congressional clerks in 1789; that the docket on the reverse of the manuscript was written by the same person who wrote the docket on President Washington's October 2, 1789, letter transmitting North Carolina's copy of the Bill of Rights to its chief executive, Gov. Samuel Johnston, and who wrote the

---

[41] Second Amended State's Memorandum of Law, Exhibits 35 (Stephen Harmelin to John L. Richardson, March 14, 2003) and 36 (commission document).

docket on President Washington's June 19, 1789, letter to Governor Johnston and the Council of State; and that the document was therefore the same copy of the Bill of Rights that President Washington sent to and that was received by the State of North Carolina in 1789.

After examination of the Bill of Rights, Dr. Bowling informed a representative of the NCC that it was one of the original handwritten copies of the Bill of Rights, and that it was North Carolina's copy. On February 12, 2003, Dr. Bowling wrote to Seth Kaller, a New York antiquities dealer associated with Pratt, expressing his opinion and the collective opinion of the staff of the FFC Project, that the document was an authentic copy of the Bill of Rights and "is without question the North Carolina copy."[42]

On or about February 26, 2003, Stephen Harmelin, general counsel for the NCC, met with Pratt and Richardson in New York City to discuss the proposed purchase of the Bill of Rights. Because of Dr. Bowling's opinion that the copy of the Bill of Rights being offered for sale was the copy originally sent to North Carolina, the NCC wanted to involve the State in any acquisition of the document. Kaller and Reese supported the NCC's position, while Richardson strongly resisted the suggestion. The meeting ended without a purchase agreement and with Richardson demanding possession of the document from Reese, who had it at the time.

Shortly thereafter, Joseph Torsella, president of the NCC, notified the governors of Pennsylvania and North Carolina that the NCC had been contacted about purchasing what was believed to be North Carolina's copy of the Bill of Rights. State officials contacted the United States Attorney's Office (USAO) and the Federal Bureau of Investigation (FBI). The USAO and FBI began making plans to recover the document.

Recovery of a Stolen Treasure

On March 13, 2003, the United States District Court for the Eastern District of North Carolina issued a seizure warrant for North Carolina's copy of the Bill of Rights on probable cause to believe that the document was subject to forfeiture to the United States as stolen property.[43] The same day, two FBI special agents of the Philadelphia Division requested that Torsella and Harmelin help the FBI recover the Bill of Rights. They agreed on behalf of the NCC and, with the cooperation of Reese and Tillou, took action to prevent the expiration of the two-month options to sell the document, given to them by Pratt. Tillou assigned his option to Reese, who assigned the joint option to the NCC.

Under the guidance of the FBI, the NCC continued to negotiate what was now a sham sale with Richardson, who was acting as attorney-in-fact for Pratt.

---

[42] Second Amended State's Memorandum of Law, Exhibit 40 (Kenneth R. Bowling to Seth Kaller, February 12, 2003).

[43] The seizure warrant was issued pursuant to 18 U.S.C. §§ 981(a)(1)(C) and 982, and 28 U.S.C. § 2461(c).

Pratt, who believed the negotiations and pending sale to be legitimate, executed in Colorado, as principal for himself and WPI, a general power of attorney in favor of Richardson. The power of attorney authorized Richardson to act in Pratt's "place and stead in any way which [Pratt] could do if . . . personally present with respect to the completion of the purchase by the National Constitution Center of an original manuscript of the Bill of Rights and the sale thereof by [Pratt]."[44]

On March 18, 2003, the FBI assembled a team of agents in Harmelin's law offices, where the sale was to take place. Kaller and Torsella were also present. Torsella brought a check for $4,000,000 from the NCC made payable to Richardson's law firm for "Acc. of Bill of Rights." Richardson was authorized by the firm to accept delivery of the check.

Richardson arrived at the closing without the Bill of Rights. When he was satisfied with the closing documents, he called a courier on his cellular phone to bring the manuscript into Harmelin's law offices. The courier had picked up the document from his employer, WPI, in Connecticut and transported it to Philadelphia, spending the night in New Jersey. The courier entered the office with the Bill of Rights and set it on the table. Kaller examined the Bill of Rights to verify that it was the document to be purchased. Upon Harmelin's signal that the Bill of Rights was present, FBI agents entered the room with badges, identified themselves, and recovered the manuscript. Richardson was listed on the return of the seizure warrant and the FBI's standard form for acknowledging the seizure of property as the person from whom the Bill of Rights was recovered.

On March 30, 2003, the United States filed a complaint for forfeiture *in rem* against "North Carolina's Original Copy of the Bill of Rights" in the United States District Court for the Eastern District of North Carolina.[45] On or about April 1, the document was placed in the custody of the United States Marshal for the Eastern District of North Carolina. When the Bill of Rights was brought to Raleigh for the forfeiture proceeding, George Stevenson Jr., a senior archivist at the North Carolina Office of Archives and History, examined the manuscript. Stevenson, who is an expert in the authentication of manuscripts created during the federal period, concluded that, in his opinion, the recovered manuscript was authentic and the same document that President Washington had sent to Governor Johnston in 1789.

The United States, the State of North Carolina, Robert Vires Matthews, Wayne Pratt, and WPI, all claimed ownership of the Bill of Rights in the federal forfeiture action. During the litigation, however, Wayne Pratt and WPI conveyed to the State all interests they had in the Bill of Rights. The State accepted the conveyance, but maintained that "it alone had and continues to have title to [the Bill of Rights]." Thereafter on September 10, 2003, the United States filed a

---

[44] Second Amended State's Memorandum of Law, Exhibit 43 (general power of attorney).
[45] See *United States v. North Carolina's Original Copy of the Bill of Rights*, No. 5:03-CV-2040BO (E.D.N.C. Feb. 19, 2004), *vacated, In re Matthews*, 395 F.3d at 477 (4th Cir. 2005). An action *in rem* (literally, "with respect to the thing") involves the determination of proprietary title to property.

State Highway Patrol officers deliver the Bill of Rights to the State Archives on August 4, 2005, hours after the manuscript was returned to state officials in a ceremony at the nearby State Capitol. Jeffrey J. Crow and Staci Meyer, deputy secretaries of the Department of Cultural Resources, escort the document. Image courtesy of the State Archives, N.C. Office of Archives and History, Raleigh.

notice of voluntary dismissal of the civil forfeiture action against the document. Notwithstanding the dismissal of the action, the district court concluded that it had *in rem* jurisdiction to issue a ruling on the merits. Relying on *State v. West* (1977), the district court concluded that the Original Copy of the Bill of Rights, as an official document, belonged to the State of North Carolina.[46] Matthews appealed.

The United States Court of Appeals for the Fourth Circuit held that the district court "lacked authority to determine ownership rights in the document after the voluntary dismissal."[47] The Fourth Circuit vacated the district court order granting ownership and possession of the document to the State and remanded with instructions for the district court to "restore the parties, as closely as possible, to the status quo ante as it determines that phrase to mean." The court specifically cautioned, "Whatever method the district court chooses [to determine the status quo ante] should fully preserve the parties' ability to pursue their ownership claims in other proceedings."[48]

Upon remand, the district court concluded that the "status quo ante" meant "the moment of time immediately prior to the seizure of the document by federal agents. . . ." The district court determined that the party with the present right to control the property had the superior possessory interest. Richardson had constructive possession of the Bill of Rights on behalf of WPI just before the seizure. The district court concluded, however, that because Pratt and WPI conveyed their interests in the Bill of Rights to the State on September 10, 2003,

[46] 31 N.C. App. at 431, 229 S.E.2d at 826 (1976), *aff'd*, 293 N.C. at 18, 235 S.E.2d at 150 (1977).
[47] *United States v. Matthews (In re Matthews)*, 395 F.3d at 477, 478-480 (4th Cir. 2005).
[48] *United States v. Matthews (In re Matthews)*, 395 F.3d at 477, 483-484 (4th Cir. 2005).

"any interest which Richardson, Pratt and WPI ha[d] in the Bill of Rights, including any possessory interest, passed to the State of North Carolina on September 10, 2003, and was not affected by the voluntary dismissal." On August 4, 2005, the district court ordered that the United States marshal return possession of the Bill of Rights to the State by "immediately delivering it to the Governor of North Carolina or his legal designee."[49] The same day, Governor Easley ordered the document placed in the State Archives, where it remains today. Matthews again appealed, but the Fourth Circuit affirmed the district court's decision.[50]

THE STATE'S CASE FOR OWNERSHIP

AUTHORS' NOTE: Although the State regained *possession* of its copy of the Bill of Rights through federal litigation, those proceedings could not be used to establish clear legal title to the manuscript against those who claimed, or might claim in the future, an ownership interest in it. To obtain unassailable clear title to the manuscript, the State pursued a civil action in state superior court to obtain a judicial declaration that the State had superior legal title to its copy of the Bill of Rights. The remainder of this essay is an edited version of the argument made in the memorandum of law that the State submitted in state court to support its claim of *ownership* in the Bill of Rights. Although the argument incorporates much of the historical evidence presented in the preceding section, it primarily addresses the issues of law raised in the lawsuit and provides additional contemporaneous evidence supporting the State's claim of ownership of the Bill of Rights.

The 1977 replevin case, *State of North Carolina v. B. C. West Jr.*, controlled the disposition of this action.[51] Under *West*, the State is entitled to a declaration that the Bill of Rights is a public document owned by the State, provided it establishes the authenticity of the Bill of Rights and its presence in public custody; that the Bill of Rights was required by law to be permanently retained; the presumption that public officials have properly performed their duty is overcome; and that the Bill of Rights was in a public archive from which it was stolen or otherwise improperly removed.[52]

In determining whether the State carried its burden of proof, the *West* courts applied the principles of North Carolina law that public records and documents are the property of the State, and title to them cannot be transferred to any private individual other than by act of the legislature;[53] and that a person taking

---

[49] *United States v. North Carolina's Original Copy of the Bill of Rights*, No. 5:03-CV-204 (E.D. N.C. Aug. 4, 2005), *aff'd*, *United States v. Matthews*, No. 05-2095, slip op. (4th Cir. June 22, 2006).

[50] See *United States v. Matthews*, No. 05-2095 (4th Cir. May 24, 2006) (unpublished); 2006 U.S. App. LEXIS 15717.

[51] *State v. West*, 31 N.C. App. at 431, 229 S.E.2d at 826 (1976), *aff'd*, 293 N.C. at 18, 235 S.E.2d at 150 (1977).

[52] *State v. West*, 31 N.C. App. at 437, 229 S.E.2d at 829.

[53] *State v. West*, 31 N.C. App. at 441, 229 S.E.2d at 831 (citing *United States v. Mallery*, 53 F. Supp. 564 [1944]).

public records into his possession, or a subsequent purchaser for value from him, whether on the open market or otherwise, does not acquire good title, but is, in fact, liable as a converter, regardless of his having acted in good faith.[54]

North Carolina law is absolutely clear that private individuals cannot acquire title to public records of the State absent an act of the legislature.[55] "Public records" are

> all documents, papers, letters, . . . *made or received pursuant to law or ordinance in connection with the transaction of public business* by any agency of North Carolina government or its subdivisions. Agency . . . shall mean and include every public office, public officer or official, . . . authority or other unit of government of the State . . . (emphasis added).[56]

The phrase, "made or received pursuant to law or ordinance in connection with the transaction of public business," includes both records required by law and records retained in carrying out a lawful duty.[57]

The North Carolina Court of Appeals in *West* explicitly set out the rule of law in North Carolina:

> [p]ublic records and documents are the property of the State and not of the individual who happens, at the moment, to have them in his possession; and when they are deposited in the place designated for them by law, there they must remain, and can be *removed only under authority of an act of the Legislature and in the manner and for the purpose designated by law* (emphasis added).[58]

In *West*, the State filed suit to recover possession of two superior court indictments, drawn in 1767 and 1768, respectively, and signed by William Hooper, who later signed the Declaration of Independence on behalf of North Carolina. The indictments had been acquired by the defendant, B. C. West Jr., for valuable consideration and in good faith, from a New York gallery and had been the subjects of private sales and transfers for many years. The defendant argued, therefore, that the indictments were privately owned. The trial court agreed, concluding that absent some evidence that the indictments improperly left the possession of the superior court, the State had not overcome the presumption that the possessor in good faith had acquired title.

The court of appeals reversed, concluding that the bills of indictment became public records and state property upon being docketed in the superior court. In reversing the trial court, the court of appeals stated that there was no question about the authenticity of the documents and, therefore, examined only three of

---

[54] *State v. West*, 293 N.C. at 18, 31, 235 S.E.2d at 150, 158 (1977) (citing *Wall v. Colvard, Inc.*, 268 N.C. at 43, 149 S.E. 2d at 559 [1966]; 18 *American Jurisprudence* 2D *Conversion* § 7).

[55] *State v. West*, 31 N.C. App. at 431, 229 S.E.2d at 826 (1976), *aff'd*, 293 N.C. at 18, 235 S.E.2d at 150 (1977).

[56] N.C. Gen. Stat. § 132-1(a) (2007).

[57] *News and Observer Publ'g v. Wake County Hosp. Sys.*, 55 N.C. App. at 1, 284 S.E.2d at 542 (1981), *cert. denied*, 459 U.S. at 803, 74 L. Ed. 2d at 42 (1982).

[58] *State v. West*, 293 N.C. at 32, 235 S.E.2d at 158 (quoting 66 *American Jurisprudence* 2D *Records and Recording Laws* § 10 [1973]).

the four elements of proof required to establish the State's claim: (1) whether the documents at issue were required by law to be permanently retained; (2) whether the State had overcome the presumption that public officials properly performed their duty (i.e., in the absence of other facts, if a state official has relinquished possession of public documents, presumably he did so lawfully); and (3) whether the documents had been in the public archives and improperly removed from there. The court of appeals concluded that the State met each of the requirements and had superior rights to the indictments as against a bona fide purchaser.[59]

In *West*, the court of appeals stated that the element of whether the indictments were required by law to be retained was a question of law. The court of appeals concluded that the State had proved this element based simply on the existence of a law making criminal the unlawful removal of court and county records.[60] The court of appeals further concluded that the State had overcome the presumption that public officials had properly performed their duties, since possession of the documents by the defendant irrefutably established that some court official had not properly performed his legal duty to preserve the indictments:

> It is a well-settled principle of law that title to government property may pass only in the manner prescribed by the duly constituted legislative body and that title to any such property may not be forfeited through the oversight, carelessness, negligence, or even intentional conduct of any of the agents of the government.[61]

Finally, the court of appeals concluded that the State had carried its burden of proving that the indictments were in a public archive and were stolen or otherwise improperly removed by proving that the documents were at one time present in the records of the Salisbury District Superior Court, and that there was no evidence of abandonment or of any legal authorization for the abandonment of indictments under North Carolina law.[62] Having determined that the State had carried its burden, the court concluded that the two indictments were the property of the State to be held in trust for the public, emphasizing that:

> [s]ince ownership to the bills of indictment is in the State, it cannot be disposed of except as provided by law. It cannot be forfeited through the oversight, carelessness or even intentional conduct of any of the agents of the State. Thus, the documents in question left the custody of the court in an unlawful manner and legal title thereto cannot pass to the individual who happens, at the moment, to have them in his possession.[63]

---

[59] *State v. West*, 31 N.C. App. at 436-437, 229 S.E.2d at 829.

[60] *State v. West*, 31 N.C. App. at 437-441, 229 S.E.2d at 829-831; N.C.G.S. § 14-76 (1977).

[61] *State v. West*, 31 N.C. App. at 441, 229 S.E.2d at 831-832 (citing *United States v. Mallery*, 53 F. Supp. 564 [1944]).

[62] *State v. West*, 31 N.C. App. at 442-444, 447-448, 229 S.E.2d at 832-833, 835.

[63] *State v. West*, 31 N.C. App. at 448-449, 229 S.E.2d at 836.

In affirming the court of appeals, the North Carolina Supreme Court limited its decision to the property right of the State in documents that were public in origin.[64] The court first concluded that the change of sovereignty from the King of England to the State of North Carolina instantaneously transferred to the State—but did not alter—the right of the king to his official property.[65] The supreme court next concluded that the State had not abandoned the indictments, stating:

> [U]nauthorized removal of the documents from the office of the clerk by a third person, with or without the knowledge and consent of the clerk, *whether or not a state of unrest bordering on anarchy prevails in the community*, does not show an intent by the owner to abandon his property (emphasis added).[66]

The court concluded that the presence of other contemporaneous records in the possession of the State negated the defendant's supposition that the indictments were intentionally discarded by the clerk of court or his successor. Finally, the supreme court concluded that even if the clerk had intentionally thrown away the indictments, "such action by him would not constitute an abandonment by the sovereign of its property in the absence of a showing that the sovereign authorized it or, with knowledge of it, ratified it."[67]

The principles of law applied in the *West* cases are consistent with the law in other jurisdictions regarding title to public documents.[68] Federal courts have likewise concluded that good title to stolen property of the United States cannot pass to a private purchaser for value, even when acquired in good faith.[69] The applicable law regarding public records has been summarized in the second edition of *American Jurisprudence* as follows:

> Also, because public records and documents are the property of the state and not of the individual who has them in his or her possession, the custodian of a public record cannot destroy it, deface it, or give it up without authority from the same source that required the record to be made.[70]

The law is therefore clear that public documents are the property of the State, and that public records of North Carolina cannot be legally removed, nor title transferred, without authorization from the General Assembly. This statement of North Carolina law applies with equal force to all of the State's public records—be they an indictment from 1767 or a manuscript copy of the Bill of Rights from 1789. Accordingly, North Carolina law entitles the State to the

---

[64] *State v. West*, 293 N.C. at 25-26, 235 S.E.2d at 154.

[65] *State v. West*, 293 N.C. at 27, 29, 235 S.E.2d at 155, 156.

[66] *State v. West*, 293 N.C. at 30-31, 235 S.E.2d at 157.

[67] *State v. West*, 293 N.C. at 31-32, 235 S.E.2d at 157-158.

[68] See *Mayor of New York v. Lent*, 51 Barb. at 19 (N.Y. Gen. Term 1868); *De La O v. Acoma*, 1 N.M. at 226 (N.M. 1857); *Morris's Appeal*, 68 Pa. at 16 (1871).

[69] *United States v. Barnard*, 72 F. Supp. at 531 (D. Tenn. 1947).

[70] *American Jurisprudence* 2D *Records and Recording Laws* § 11, at 63-64 (2001).

judicial declaration that the manuscript Bill of Rights now in the custody of the State Archives is a public record of this State, and that the State's ownership rights are superior to those of all other persons and entities.

The manuscript Bill of Rights is one of the original handwritten copies prepared by Congress in 1789 and is the manuscript sent to and received by North Carolina.

The manuscript Bill of Rights is one of the handwritten copies of the twelve amendments to the United States Constitution, prepared at the direction of Congress in 1789 and transmitted by President Washington for ratification to the executives of the eleven states that had ratified the Constitution and to the executives of Rhode Island and North Carolina, which had not yet ratified. There is undisputed evidence to establish this fact.

Dr. Kenneth R. Bowling is a researcher, author, and compiler of historical manuscripts at the First Federal Congress Project. Dr. Bowling's expertise is in the area of federal records and documents of the revolutionary and early national periods, specifically those of the First Federal Congress. In February 2003, a representative of the National Constitution Center in Philadelphia requested Dr. Bowling to attempt to authenticate a manuscript being offered for sale to the NCC and purported to be one of the handwritten copies of the Bill of Rights. Dr. Bowling examined photographs of the front and reverse of the manuscript, including its docket. He concluded that not only was the manuscript one of the original handwritten copies of the Bill of Rights prepared by Congress, but it was also the specific document that President Washington had sent to Governor Johnston in 1789. He reached his conclusion by comparing the pattern, general style of the endorsement, and specific characteristics of the handwriting of the docket on the reverse of the manuscript Bill of Rights with dockets on other documents known to have been written by North Carolina government clerks of the same period. Dr. Bowling prepared a letter of authenticity dated February 12, 2003, for the manuscript Bill of Rights in which he expressed his opinion that the document "is without question the North Carolina copy of the Bill of Rights."

George Stevenson Jr., senior archivist for the North Carolina Office of Archives and History, has examined and accurately authenticated manuscripts and other papers from the colonial and federal periods "dozens of times." He is an expert in the areas of identification and authentication of records, documents, and manuscripts made and received by government officers and agencies from the colonial through the federal periods of North Carolina history, and in the record-keeping practices of state officers and agencies during the federal period. In April 2003, Stevenson was requested to examine at the United States marshal's office in Raleigh and attempt to authenticate a manuscript purported to be an original copy of the Bill of Rights. The document was the one recovered in Philadelphia from John Richardson, agent for Wayne Pratt and WPI, during the staged sale of the manuscript to the National Constitution Center. Stevenson thoroughly examined the front and reverse of the manuscript. The endorsement on the back read:

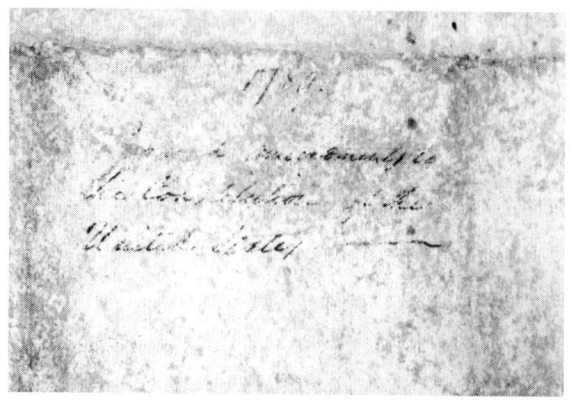

1789
Proposed amendments to
the Constitution of the
United States

After examining the document, Stevenson had "no doubt" that it was an authentic manuscript of the Bill of Rights prepared by Congress in 1789, and the same manuscript received by Governor Johnston in 1789 and subsequently transmitted to and permanently retained by the General Assembly. He reached this conclusion using two separate methods: his knowledge of the record-keeping practices of state officers and agencies, including the governor, Council of State, and General Assembly, at the time President Washington sent a manuscript copy of the Bill of Rights to Governor Johnston; and his lay opinion that the handwriting of the docket on the reverse of the Bill of Rights was the same as on the dockets on other records known to have been made or received by state agencies during the same general period.

When Stevenson first examined the manuscript Bill of Rights at the United States marshal's office, he knew that the General Assembly was the only branch of the North Carolina government that had the authority to ratify or reject proposed amendments to the federal Constitution. He expected, therefore, that any endorsement on the reverse of the manuscript received by North Carolina would have been made by the principal clerk of either the North Carolina Senate or House of Commons, but it was not.

Nevertheless, Stevenson knew that the manuscript Bill of Rights had been laid before the General Assembly and ratified, and that it would have been endorsed by some assembly clerk before it was filed and stored. With this knowledge, he returned to the State Archives with a photograph of the endorsement on the manuscript Bill of Rights to search for samples of endorsements written by other clerks in the General Assembly during the period that the Bill of Rights had been received, so that he could compare the endorsements he found to the endorsement on the manuscript. He also knew that the manuscript Bills of Rights sent to the executives of the states that had ratified the Constitution and to the executives of North Carolina and Rhode Island were not sent with an endorsement.

Stevenson first looked at the endorsement on the reverse of North Carolina's original manuscript of the Eleventh Amendment to the United States Constitution, received in 1794 and retained since that time in the state's archives. The endorsement on the proposed amendment would have been written by a legislative clerk in the 1794-1795 session of the General Assembly, which considered and ratified the amendment. The reverse of the Eleventh Amendment contains an endorsement with the following handwritten words:

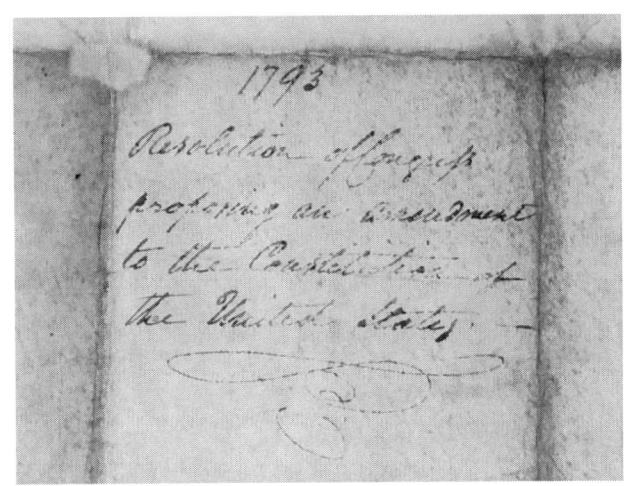

1793
Resolution of Congress proposing an amendment to the Constitution of the United States

Upon comparing this endorsement with the one on the reverse of the manuscript Bill of Rights, Stevenson concluded they were "very, very similar" in style. He logically concluded that if one person had written both endorsements, that person must have been employed by the General Assembly in both the 1789-1790 and 1794-1795 sessions. Stevenson determined by reference to the record of allowances, or budget, of the two sessions that only three assistant clerks were employed by both—Montfort Stokes, Richard Freear, and Pleasant Henderson.

Stevenson next compared the style of the endorsement on the manuscript Bill of Rights to the "format" or "style" of endorsements on other documents in the State Archives from the period, including the October 2, 1789, letter from George Washington transmitting the manuscript Bill of Rights to Gov. Samuel Johnston; the 1789 resolves of Congress that also had been transmitted with President Washington's letter; and a July 27, 1783, letter from Gov. Alexander Martin to the Council of State. Governor Martin's letter was unusual in that it appeared to be written and endorsed by the same person. He concluded that the "format" or "style" of all the endorsements was very similar.

Stevenson then consulted the estimate of allowances and other records in the State Archives to determine if a single person had been employed as a clerk of the General Assembly during the 1789-1790 session when the George Washington letter, the resolves of Congress, and the manuscript Bill of Rights were endorsed; as a clerk of the General Assembly during the 1794-1795 session when the Eleventh Amendment was endorsed; and as private secretary to the governor and secretary to the Council of State in 1783, when the Martin letter was written and endorsed. Pleasant Henderson, a longtime state employee, was the only person who was employed in these capacities during the relevant periods and therefore the only person who would have been in a position to have endorsed each of the documents.

Henderson was private secretary to Governor Martin from April 22, 1782, to May 12, 1784, and secretary to the Council of State from July 23, 1781, to September 19, 1782, and again from May 9, 1783, to November 20, 1784. Henderson was also an engrossing clerk in the General Assembly from 1786 to 1790, and an assistant clerk to the House of Commons in 1788 and from 1791 to 1796. None of the other principal clerks or assistant clerks served in all of these capacities.

Stevenson also examined the manner in which President Washington's letter, the manuscript Bill of Rights, and the resolves of Congress had been folded. In his opinion, and to a reasonable degree of historical and archival certainty, all three documents were folded in a manner consistent with the record-keeping practices of the North Carolina General Assembly during the federal period. He concluded, therefore, that based upon the similarity of style in which the endorsements on the manuscript Bill of Rights, the Eleventh Amendment, the George Washington letter, the resolves of Congress, and the Alexander Martin letter were written, and the manner in which the Bill of Rights, the George Washington letter, and the resolves of Congress were folded, that in his opinion and to a reasonable degree of historical and archival certainty the manuscript Bill of Rights was received and stored by the General Assembly during its 1789-1790 session.

Stevenson also concluded that the Bill of Rights was the manuscript received by North Carolina based upon his lay opinion that the person who endorsed the George Washington letter and the resolves of Congress was the same person who endorsed the Bill of Rights. Stevenson can recognize Pleasant Henderson's handwriting from seeing it in the assembly records in the State Archives. His opinion is that the manuscript Bill of Rights was "without question, received by the State of North Carolina in 1789 and made part of the official records of the General Assembly."

Stevenson's lay opinion that the handwriting of the endorsement on the manuscript Bill of Rights was written by a clerk for the assembly's 1789-1790 session has been confirmed by a handwriting analysis and comparison expert. R. Ken Martin is a North Carolina State Bureau of Investigation special agent and questioned documents examiner in the Questioned Documents Unit, Documents and Digital Evidence Section of the bureau's crime laboratory in Raleigh. In January 2007, Martin was assigned to conduct an analysis of the handwriting of the docket on the reverse of the manuscript Bill of Rights and to compare it with the handwriting of dockets on the reverse of four other manuscripts in the possession of the State Archives known to have been received or created by state government agencies. The four other dockets were on a 1793 report of commissioners to settle accounts; the 1794 Eleventh Amendment; the 1789 resolves of Congress; and the October 2, 1789, George Washington letter. High-resolution digital images of each docket were submitted to Martin to be analyzed and compared.

Martin examined and compared the digital images in early 2007. He subsequently went to the State Archives to examine the original docket on the manuscript Bill of Rights presented as the questioned handwriting and the original dockets presented as the known standards of handwriting. He was not able to examine the original docket on the reverse of the Bill of Rights because the manuscript upon which the docket is written had been placed in a sealed viewing container that does not allow the docket to be seen. He was not able to examine the original docket on the Eleventh Amendment for the same reason. He was, however, able to examine the original dockets on the other three manuscripts. Based upon his analysis and comparison of the digital images of all of the dockets and three of the original dockets presented as known samples, Martin concluded that, in his opinion, and to a reasonable degree of scientific certainty, the author of the known materials "very probably" wrote the questioned docket on the reverse of the manuscript Bill of Rights.

As previously noted, prior to the March 18, 2003, recovery of the Bill of Rights, five states were missing their copies: Georgia, Maryland, New York, North Carolina, and Pennsylvania. The text of the manuscript Bill of Rights differs from the known text of the copies received by Georgia, Maryland, New York, and Pennsylvania. However, the text of the manuscript matches that of the Bill of Rights received by North Carolina in 1789. The text of Article the Eighth in the manuscript Bill of Rights states in pertinent part: "In all criminal prosecutions, the accused shall enjoy the right to a speedy and public trial, by an impartial jury of the State and district *where* the Crime shall have been committed . . ." (emphasis added). The text of the eighth article in the original copies received by Georgia, Maryland, New York, and Pennsylvania states that the accused shall enjoy the right to a speedy and public trial by an impartial jury of the state and district "wherein" the crime shall have been committed.

North Carolina state archivist Jesse R. Lankford Jr. compared the language in records documenting North Carolina's ratification of the first twelve proposed amendments. North Carolina's official publication of the legislative acts of 1789 contains the text of "An Act to ratify the Amendments to the Constitution of the United States," which includes the text of the proposed amendments considered and ratified by the North Carolina General Assembly on December 22, 1789. The text of "Art. VIII" of the enrolled act uses the word "where."[71] Lankford also examined a copy of the amendments attached to Governor Martin's May 25, 1790, letter to President Washington transmitting the state's act ratifying the amendments. Governor Martin's letter, with the act ratifying the amendments, is maintained in the National Archives. "Article VIII" of the act also uses the word "where." The wording of the manuscript Bill of Rights matches the wording of North Carolina's act ratifying the amendments and Iredell's *Laws of North Carolina* in that all three use the word "where" in the eighth article.

Lankford examined historical records from Georgia, Maryland, New York, and Pennsylvania to determine whether these states had transcribed the text of the proposed amendments received by their executives and found that they had. "Article the Eighth" of Maryland's legislation ratifying the proposed amendments states in pertinent part: "In all criminal prosecutions, the accused shall

[71] Iredell, *Laws of the State of North Carolina*, 672-673.

enjoy the right to a speedy and public trial by an impartial jury of the state and district *wherein* the crime shall have been committed . . ." (emphasis added). Similar documents or manuscripts from Georgia, New York, and Pennsylvania also used the word "wherein." Lankford concluded that the difference in wording between the proposed amendments in the possession of the State Archives and the proposed amendments received by Georgia, Maryland, New York, and Pennsylvania "establishes beyond a reasonable doubt that the Archives Document is the same document received by North Carolina governor Samuel Johnston in 1789."

North Carolina's copy of the Bill of Rights was required by law to be permanently retained.

The test set forth by the court of appeals in *West* requires that the State prove that the record in question was required by law to be permanently retained. This is a question of law, not of fact. The duty to permanently retain public records may be imposed by either statutory or common law.[72] The state has a long history of requiring—by common law or statute—public officials to permanently retain the state's records. Original records in the State Archives dating back to at least 1708 establish that North Carolina has complied with its duty to preserve original government records. The records are arranged by record group for all of the principal offices of the state created under the North Carolina constitutions of 1776, 1868, and 1971. One record group contains the records of the North Carolina General Assembly.

The North Carolina General Assembly consists of two houses. The upper house is known as the senate. The lower house has had several names since the colonial period, including the House of Burgesses, House of Commons, and House of Representatives. The lower house of North Carolina's General Assembly had a common law duty to permanently retain its records, derived from the British common law, which was incorporated whole cloth by statute into North Carolina state law in 1778, unless destructive of, repugnant to, or inconsistent with the independence of the state.

The British House of Commons was, during the colonial period, a court of record. George Stevenson Jr., senior archivist at the North Carolina State Archives, defines a court of record as "any court whose proceedings are reduced to writing as a perpetual memorial."[73] The British House of Commons was a court of record because it had the power of judicature in some cases. Specifically, the House of Commons could judge the validity of election returns electing members to Parliament, could determine who was entitled to be a member of the House of Commons, and had the power to require the great seal to be affixed to a

---

[72] *State v. West*, 31 N.C. App. at 437, 441, 229 S.E.2d at 829, 831.
[73] *Accord West*, 31 N.C. App. at 439, 229 S.E.2d at 830 (citing Blackstone).

document.[74] As a court of record, the House of Commons required parliamentary clerks to preserve the records of that house and not let them out of their custody.

The North Carolina House of Commons was a court of record in exactly the same way. Accordingly, the House had a duty to permanently preserve records during North Carolina's colonial (1663-1776), revolutionary (1776-1783), federal (1783-1815), and antebellum (1815-1861) periods. According to Stevenson, this duty was based on four factors:

> ... [T]he first being that they from their earliest days considered themselves a reflection of the House of Commons in Great Britain and modeled themselves and claimed the same rights as the House of Commons in Great Britain.
>
> And the second is the definition of Sir Edward Coke as to their being a court of record requiring them therefore to keep a permanent record. And the third thing, the records themselves have survived and testimony within the records indicates they considered their records—records; their archives—records, and permanent records at that.
>
> And the last thing is simply this consideration, that here you have a branch of government, the legislative branch of government, whose action or inaction so nearly touches the life, liberty, and property of every citizen that it's axiomatic that the archives of such a body as that would be permanent records.[75]

Since at least the 1760s, North Carolina's legislative clerks have been required to keep and protect the records of the General Assembly. Evidence of this duty is found in a November 19, 1788, memorial submitted to the House of Commons by John Hunt, clerk of the House since April 1777. In that petition, Hunt declared:

> James Green Esquire, now deceased, lodged in [my] hands, the papers of the three Provincial Conventions and those of the Council of Safety, that had happened prior to [my] said appointment, which were then numerous, that since they have become much more so, that during almost Twelve years [I have] been in possession of these papers [I] never [have] been allowed one Shilling either for office rent or any Copy furnished or search made, the applications for recourse to, and Copies have been made almost innumerable as well between as at the different assemblies.

Hunt further described the considerable burden placed upon the clerk in whose custody the records remained:

> That the General Assembly having thought proper to hold their Sessions at sundry different places in the State, by which it became his duty to remove these papers to the different places which they thought proper to assemble at, so deranged them that it took considerable time & pains to file them in order again. . . . During the whole of this time no person but himself alone has had access to these papers.

The Committee on Revenue allowed Hunt twenty-five pounds for his services.[76]

---

[74] John Hatsell, ed., *Precedents of Proceedings in the House of Commons*, 3d ed., 4 vols. (London: printed for T. Payne, 1796), 2:151, 237-260.

[75] Second Amended State's Memorandum of Law, Exhibit 124 (deposition of George Stevenson).

[76] Committee on Revenue report re. memorial of John Hunt, December 1, 1788, General Assembly Session Records, Nov.-Dec. 1788, Box 1, North Carolina State Archives.

Hunt's petition establishes that preservation of the assembly's records was so important that only the clerk could access them. This petition also demonstrates that the clerk from the colonial period, James Green, preserved the papers of the House of Commons during that period. Upon Green's death, the papers were transferred to the successor clerk, John Hunt, who preserved the records into the federal period.

The common law requirement to preserve public records has been codified by the General Assembly since at least the federal period. On December 20, 1787, two years before the Bill of Rights was received by Governor Johnston and laid before the assembly, the North Carolina House of Commons passed a resolution regarding the preservation of records of the General Assembly, stating:

> [W]hereas the official dispatches laid before the General Assembly remain in the office of the clerks of the two houses after the rising of the session, *and it is necessary that they should be preserved*:
>
> *Resolved*, That the clerks of the two houses be and they are hereby required, after the rising of each session of the General Assembly, *to lodge in the Secretary's office all such official dispatches as may remain in their respective offices or possession* (emphases added).[77]

The North Carolina Senate concurred:

> Received also a resolution directing the clerks of the Assembly to *deliver to the Secretary of State all dispatches from Congress and other important papers* in their possession; which was read, concurred with and returned (emphasis added).[78]

In 1812, the General Assembly ratified "An Act directing the duties of the Secretary of State in certain cases, and more effectually to provide for the safe keeping of the Public Records, Books and Documents." The act of 1812 required the secretary of state to collect and bind "the Acts and Journals of Congress, together with the Public Documents received from the Executive and the Congress of the United States." The statute further required the secretary of state to catalogue and preserve the books, documents, laws, acts, and journals collected by him.[79]

The collection, organization, and preservation of public documents continued through the antebellum period. The 1836-1837 *Revised Statutes of North Carolina* directed the clerks of both legislative houses, at the close of each session, to "deposit in the office of the secretary of state the journals of the legislature."[80] In February 1857, the General Assembly passed a resolution requiring the assistant clerks of the senate and House of Commons to collect and arrange in the archives of each house all of their records and papers located in various places in the

---

[77] Journal of the House of Commons, 1787 (microfilm copy in the State Library of North Carolina, title page and publication data missing), p. 49.

[78] Journal of the Senate, 1787 (microfilm copy in the State Library of North Carolina, title page and publication data missing), p. 46.

[79] Laws of the State of North Carolina, 1812, ch. XVI, § 1 (microfiche copy in the State Library of North Carolina, title page and publication data missing), p. 14.

[80] *The Revised Statutes of the State of North Carolina*, 2 vols. (Raleigh: Turner and Hughes, 1837), 1:301.

Capitol. The resolution further required the clerks of each house to collect and have bound or otherwise preserved legislative documents in order to establish a library of documents in each house.[81] These laws, resolutions, and statutes clearly include the Bill of Rights as a public record of the State required by law to be permanently retained.

The State has overcome the presumption that public officials lawfully relinquished possession of the Bill of Rights.

West requires the State to overcome the presumption that public officials performed their duties as required by law; that is, to permanently retain state records and allow them to be "removed only under authority of an act of the Legislature and in the manner and for the purpose designated by law."[82] Generally, public officials are presumed to perform their duties as required by law. The presumption, however, is "rebuttable by affirmative evidence of irregularity or failure to perform [a] duty."[83]

In *West*, the court of appeals concluded that the State overcame the presumption that court officials lawfully relinquished possession of the indictments by showing only that a statute required the indictments to be preserved, and that they were found in the defendant's possession. The court of appeals stated, "It is obvious . . . that some court official has not properly performed his *statutory and common law* duty with regard to the preservation of these indictments *since they are now found in the hands of defendant*" (emphases added).[84]

In this case, the presumption is that public officials properly performed their duty to either permanently retain the Bill of Rights or relinquish custody and possession of the document if directed to do so by law. The State's evidence is undisputed that the Bill of Rights was required by statutory and common law to be permanently retained as a record of the General Assembly. The State's evidence is also undisputed that the Bill of Rights was recovered from the possession of John Richardson, Wayne Pratt's attorney-in-fact. In *West*, the court of appeals concluded that evidence that North Carolina law required public officials to permanently retain court records, along with evidence that the records were found in the custody of someone else, was sufficient to overcome the presumption that public officials lawfully relinquished possession of the indictments. In this instance, the State's evidence that the Bill of Rights was required to be permanently retained by the General Assembly and evidence that

---

[81] *Public Laws of the State of North-Carolina Passed by the General Assembly at the Session of 1856-'57* (Raleigh: Holden and Wilson, 1857), 70.

[82] *State v. West*, 31 N.C. App. at 437, 229 S.E.2d at 829, 293 N.C. at 32, 235 S.E.2d at 158 (quoting 66 *American Jurisprudence* 2D *Records and Recording Laws* § 10).

[83] *Huntley v. Potter*, 255 N.C. at 619, 628, 122 S.E.2d at 681, 687 (1961).

[84] *State v. West*, 31 N.C. App. at 441, 229 S.E.2d at 831.

it was possessed by John Richardson meet the standard established by the court of appeals for proving this element.[85]

There is no evidence that the General Assembly of North Carolina has ever authorized transfer of title to its copy of the Bill of Rights. Furthermore, the court of appeals stated in *West* that "there has never been a legally authorized means of selling, forfeiting or abandoning public documents of the State of North Carolina."[86] As in *West*, it is obvious that some government official has not properly performed his statutory and/or common law duty to permanently retain the Bill of Rights because it was found in the hands of John Richardson.[87]

The State has presented affirmative evidence of irregularity sufficient to overcome the presumption that public officials lawfully relinquished possession of the Bill of Rights.[88] The State has also established that documents related or similar to the Bill of Rights still are permanently retained in the State Archives. In *West*, the court of appeals concluded that such evidence was sufficient to show that the indictments were stolen or improperly removed from the public archive.[89] The North Carolina Supreme Court concluded that the same evidence also tends to negate the supposition that public officials abandoned or otherwise lawfully relinquished possession of the indictments.[90] The State contends, based on the state supreme court's application of this evidence in *West*, that evidence of other, contemporaneous documents related or similar to the Bill of Rights being permanently retained in the State Archives also shows irregularity sufficient to overcome the presumption that public officials performed their duties as required by law.[91]

The resolves of Congress and the October 2, 1789, George Washington letter transmitting the Bill of Rights have been continuously retained by public officials and are preserved in the State Archives today. The letter from President Washington was filed and permanently retained in the records of the General Assembly from its receipt until it was transferred to the custody of the North Carolina Historical Commission, predecessor of the State Archives, on March 18, 1915. The resolves of Congress, requiring the proposed amendments to be transmitted to the states, Rhode Island, and North Carolina, were sent with the Bill of Rights and were filed and permanently retained in the records of the General Assembly from receipt until transferred to the custody of the North Carolina Historical Commission during the 1916-1918 biennium. Of the documents transmitted to the state in 1789, only the manuscript Bill of Rights was missing from the state's archives.

---

[85] *State v. West*, 31 N.C. App. at 443, 229 S.E.2d at 832-833.

[86] *State v. West*, 31 N.C. App. at 446, 229 S.E.2d at 834.

[87] See *West*, 31 N.C. App. at 441, 229 S.E.2d at 831.

[88] See *Huntley v. Potter*, 255 N.C. at 619, 628, 122 S.E.2d at 681, 687 (1961).

[89] *State v. West*, 31 N.C. App. at 443, 229 S.E.2d at 833.

[90] *State v. West*, 293 N.C. at 31, 235 S.E.2d at 157.

[91] See *Huntley*, 255 N.C. at 628, 122 S.E.2d at 687.

Furthermore, the proposed Eleventh Amendment to the United States Constitution was received by North Carolina during the 1794-1795 session of the General Assembly and thereafter made a part of the official records of the General Assembly. At the end of the session, the manuscript was folded, endorsed, and stored in a manner similar to the Bill of Rights. Today, the Eleventh Amendment remains preserved as a public record in the State Archives.

The first issue of the United States Constitution, the certified printed copy ordered on September 28, 1787, to be sent to the states for ratification, is also preserved in the State Archives. The first issue of the Constitution was permanently retained in the papers of the secretary of state, the custodian of records of constitutional conventions, from its receipt until transferred to the predecessor of the State Archives in 1919. The permanent retention of these documents, related or similar to the Bill of Rights, contradicts any assertion that the State expressly abandoned the Bill of Rights during secession, or impliedly abandoned the manuscript merely by seceding.

The existence in the State Archives of documents related to the ratification of the Bill of Rights provides additional evidence that overcomes the presumption that public officials lawfully relinquished possession of the Bill of Rights. The following records, which document the ratification process of the Bill of Rights from the time the manuscript was received through the transmittal of the act ratifying the Bill of Rights to the president, have been continuously retained by public officials in the state's archives:

(1) November 4, 1789, message from the North Carolina House of Commons to Gov. Samuel Johnston: The message informs the governor that "[t]he General Assembly are now formed and ready to receive from your Excellency such public papers and dispatches as you may have to lay before them for their Consideration."[92]

(2) Governor Johnston's response to the House of Commons message: The governor states that he was sending all of the public papers and dispatches received by him since the last session of the General Assembly:

Gentlemen, in pursuance of your Message of Yesterday,[93] I send you all the Publick Papers, and Dispatches which have been received by me, since the last Session of the General Assembly; which, with the Journal of the Council of State, and my Letter Book, contain all the Information which I have to lay before you at present.

Attached to the message was a list of papers. The first numbered item on the list includes "Dispatches from the President of the United States." Although the dispatches were not itemized, the Bill of Rights would have been included in the "Dispatches from the President" because the General Assembly, and no

---

[92] Journal of the House of Commons, 1789 (microfilm copy in the State Library of North Carolina, publication data missing), p. 4.

[93] The message from Governor Johnston is misdated October 5, 1789. The 1789 session of the General Assembly did not begin until November 2. Furthermore, in his message, Governor Johnston refers to the General Assembly's message of "Yesterday," meaning November 4, 1789.

other body, had the authority to ratify amendments to the United States Constitution.[94]

(3) November 5, 1789, message from the House of Commons to the senate: The House of Commons message transmitted Governor Johnston's message with the attached public papers and dispatches.[95]

(4) November 23, 1789, entry in the Journal of the House of Commons: The journal entry summarizes the daily proceedings in the House. The entry for November 23, 1789, establishes that John Hamilton of Edenton introduced a bill to ratify the proposed amendments to the Constitution. The bill was read the first time, passed, and sent to the senate. The bill was eventually passed by each house, leading to the ratification of the amendments on December 22, 1789. Although the manuscript of the ratified act was removed without authority from the State Archives, the published act remains among the volumes of the State Library of North Carolina.[96]

(5) April 11, 1790, letter from Samuel Johnston and Benjamin Hawkins to Gov. Alexander Martin: Governor Martin received from North Carolina's United States senators in New York an inquiry as to whether North Carolina had ratified the proposed amendments to the United States Constitution:

> Several of the States have sent up their ratification of the articles proposed to the Legislatures as amendments to the Constitution of the United States. We know not whether the Legislature of North Carolina ratified these or not, in either case however it is proper we should be informed of it officially. The usual conveyance to Congress is through the President.[97]

(6) May 25, 1790, response by Governor Martin to the senators: Governor Martin's reply indicates that he had sent to North Carolina secretary of state Glasgow for exemplified copies of the act ratifying the Bill of Rights:

> I was informed by some of the Clerks at the adjournment of the assembly that the ratification of the articles proposed by Congress as amendments to the Constitution of the United States by the Legislature of this State had early in the Session been sent forward to Congress before my coming into the administration, and gave myself no further trouble about it, but thinking that a duplicate of the Cession Act should go forward *lest the original might miscarry*, I sent to Col. Glasgow for the Exemplification, and he accordingly transmitted me the same *with an authenticated copy of the ratification act you mentioned* which I have done myself the honour to inclose to the President of the United States (emphases added).

[94] Gov. Samuel Johnston to House of Commons, "October" [November] 5, 1789, General Assembly Session Records, Nov.-Dec. 1789, Box 1, North Carolina State Archives.

[95] House of Commons to Senate, November 5, 1789, General Assembly Session Records, Nov.-Dec. 1789, Box 1, North Carolina State Archives.

[96] Journal of the House of Commons, 1789, p. 20.

[97] Samuel Johnston and Benjamin Hawkins to Alexander Martin, April 11, 1790, Governors' Papers, Alexander Martin, G.P. 18, p. 12, North Carolina State Archives.

Governor Martin's response is recorded in his letterbook, which was required by law to be retained by each governor. Governor Martin's cover letter to President Washington, referred to above, is also recorded in his letterbook.[98]

(7) February 17, 1790, Secretary of State Accounts Settled: The secretary of state's printing accounts and receipts for February 17, 1790, list a charge of £ 2.10 "For an *Authenticated Copy* of . . . the Act for adopting the Amendments to the federal Constitution with a Testimonial to each for Congress."[99]

It is important to note that, as with the Cession Act referred to in Governor Martin's May 25, 1790, response to the senators, a certified copy of the act ratifying the proposed amendments to the Constitution, with the proposed amendments reprinted in full, was sent to President Washington, instead of the original manuscript. This practice of sending certified copies of enrolled acts, rather than originals, is additional evidence that public records were required to be retained.

Taken together, evidence that the Bill of Rights was required to be permanently retained, the document was found in Richardson's possession, and similar or related documents have been continuously retained by State officials overcomes the presumption that public officials lawfully relinquished possession of the Bill of Rights.

The Bill of Rights was in a public archive and was stolen or otherwise improperly removed.

Under *West*, the final element the State must prove to establish its claim of ownership of the Bill of Rights as a public record is that the manuscript "[was] in a public archive and [was] stolen or otherwise improperly removed."[100] In *West*, the State proved that the indictments once were in a public archive through evidence that court docket entries related to the indictments were still in the archives, the indictments themselves existed, and the expert opinion testimony of the chief of the Records Section of the Division of Archives and History that the indictments had at one time been present in the records of the court. The court of appeals found this evidence sufficient to prove that the indictments were in a public archive. In *West*, the State offered no evidence concerning how the indictments left the court records, but that omission was not fatal to its claim. Rather, the court of appeals determined that the indictments had been stolen or improperly removed from the court's records based upon the lack of evidence that the indictments were abandoned and the absence of any legal means to abandon them under English and North Carolina law.[101]

---

[98] Alexander Martin to Samuel Johnston and Benjamin Hawkins, May 25, 1790, Governors' Letterbooks, Alexander Martin, G.L.B. 10, pp. 38-41, North Carolina State Archives.

[99] See *Annals of Congress*, 1:1024 (transmitting copy certified by secretary of state).

[100] *State v. West*, 31 N.C. App. at 437, 229 S.E.2d at 829.

[101] *State v. West*, 31 N.C. App. at 442-444, 229 S.E.2d at 832-833.

The State has presented uncontroverted evidence establishing that, after ratifying the proposed amendments, the State retained its original copy of the Bill of Rights in the public archives. State Bureau of Investigation special agent Ken Martin, an expert in handwriting analysis and comparison, has declared that it is his opinion that the person who wrote the endorsements on several manuscripts continuously retained in the State's archives since they were created or received by the General Assembly in the early federal period "very probably" was the same person who wrote the endorsement on the Bill of Rights. The State's undisputed evidence tends to establish that the Bill of Rights was placed in the legislative archives contemporaneously with George Washington's letter transmitting the Bill of Rights and the 1789 resolves of Congress to the State.

George Stevenson Jr. has stated his opinion that the Bill of Rights was placed in the archival records of the General Assembly after the close of the 1789-1790 session. His conclusion is based upon many factors, including: (1) the style in which the docket on the Bill of Rights was written is consistent with the style of dockets written on other documents placed in the General Assembly's archives during the same period that the Bill of Rights would have been archived, including President Washington's letter transmitting the Bill of Rights and the 1789 resolves of Congress; (2) the manner in which the Bill of Rights had been folded is consistent with the manner in which other documents were folded for storage in the legislative archives during the same period that the Bill of Rights would have been archived; and (3) in his lay opinion, the handwriting of the docket on the Bill of Rights is the handwriting of a legislative clerk employed at the 1789-1790 session of the General Assembly.

The State also has presented evidence that its common law and statutory law required the General Assembly to permanently retain its records, and that it did so. George Washington's 1789 letter transmitting the Bill of Rights to the State, the 1789 resolves accompanying the Bill of Rights, the legislative papers dealing with the ratification of the Bill of Rights, and the manuscript proposed Eleventh Amendment have been continuously and permanently retained in the state's archives. This undisputed evidence also tends to establish that the Bill of Rights, being a document related or similar to other documents permanently retained in the legislative archives, also was placed in the state's archives.[102]

The State also has established the physical location of the legislative archives in April-May 1865. Stevenson has indicated that prior to the construction of a permanent state government office building, the principal clerks of the colonial and early federal periods permanently maintained the assemblies' records at their homes or offices. He has further noted that state laws enacted prior to the completion of the first State House required the archival legislative records to be moved into the building, and that subsequent state law required them to be moved to the new State Capitol, where they were to be permanently retained. Raymond Beck, site manager and historian for the North Carolina State Capitol

---

[102] See *West*, 31 N.C. App. at 443, 229 S.E.2d at 833.

State Historic Site and an expert in the area of the governmental uses of the first State House and the present Capitol, has noted that just prior to the occupation of Raleigh by Union troops in April 1865, the archival legislative records were stored in the Capitol. Beck has provided his further opinion that, at the time, because of their volume, the archival records "were stored in several places in the Capitol, including the State Library, the Geologist's office, the room in the southeast corner of the Senate Gallery on the third floor, and in the Secretary of State's office on the first floor."[103]

As in *West*, the State has likewise proven that the Bill of Rights was stolen or otherwise improperly removed from a public archive through the absence of any evidence that the manuscript was abandoned, forfeited, or properly sold or disposed of, and a further showing that there was no method, under state law, for the Bill of Rights to be abandoned, forfeited, sold, or disposed of.[104] The North Carolina Court of Appeals in *West* concluded that the legislature has never authorized a disposition of public records:

> [T]he General Assembly has not authorized the sale, disposition or forfeiture of public documents or court records. Rather, it has authorized a manner in which such documents are to be maintained. Moreover, the General Assembly has not prescribed a statutory period within which the State must recover its lost or stolen public records. In addition, there has never been a legally authorized means of selling, forfeiting or abandoning public documents of the State of North Carolina.[105]

There is no evidence that the North Carolina General Assembly has ever authorized transfer of title to the Bill of Rights. There is, therefore, no law or precedent in support of the proposition that the General Assembly has ever authorized the sale or other disposition of North Carolina's copy of the Bill of Rights. Absent such support, no individual could, under any circumstances, have acquired good title to the document.

Rather than relying upon only these established principles of law, however, the State has gone further and presented additional credible evidence that tends to establish that the manuscript Bill of Rights actually was stolen or improperly removed from the State Capitol during the Union army's occupation of Raleigh in April-May 1865. The State's undisputed evidence is that the Capitol was looted by Union soldiers early during the occupation of Raleigh, and that many documents were removed from the legislative archives. State Archivist Jesse R. Lankford Jr. has offered proof that several documents taken from the legislative archives early in the occupation of Raleigh, but recently returned to the State Archives, have handwritten notations on them made by Union soldiers stating that the documents were taken from the "Hall of Records" and "Records of the State." Lankford also noted that a Union captain wrote to his wife that he took

---

[103] Second Amended State's Memorandum of Law, Exhibit 51 (deposition of Raymond Beck).
[104] *State v. West*, 31 N.C. App. at 442, 446, 229 S.E.2d at 832, 834.
[105] *State v. West*, 31 N.C. App. at 446, 229 S.Ed.2d at 834.

several legislative archival records from the Capitol, including one bill dated just three years after the Bill of Rights.

Furthermore, the State has presented uncontested credible evidence tending to establish that the Bill of Rights was among the documents stolen from the legislative archives stored in the State Capitol during the Union occupation. The primary evidence that the Bill of Rights was stolen from the State Capitol is found in a letter that Charles A. Shotwell wrote to Charles Reid, a New York City promoter and friend of Shotwell's son. In the letter, Shotwell states that his son, Grier, previously has sent to Reid a "photo-print of the parchment he has in his possession," and that he is giving Reid "a history of that parchment coming into [his] hands." The circumstances surrounding Shotwell providing his written account of how he acquired the Bill of Rights and the existence of documented historical facts corroborating almost all of the account establish that his statements are trustworthy and generally accurate. In his letter, Shotwell tells Reid:

> At the beginning of the Civil War, I was living in Ohio, near the town of Tippecanoe, and by frequent visits to that town, I became acquainted with many of the boys and young men of the town, a number of whom went into the Army. Among them was a young man that I had met again after the war was over.
>
> In the year of 1866 I was living in New York City, and came West that year to visit a sister, then living at Troy, Ohio, and I stopped off at the town of Tippecanoe, which is about six miles from Troy, Ohio. I had hoped to meet some of my boy friends of the days when I was a resident of the town, myself. I went into one of the stores of the town that day, where I met one of the boys that I had known before the war.[106]

The following documented historical facts establish the accuracy of this portion of Shotwell's account. Official state and federal maps, deeds, and vital statistics records establish that in 1860, Charles Albert Shotwell was about ten years old and living with his father, Eli Shotwell, his mother, and six siblings, one of whom was his twenty-one-year-old sister, Emeline, in Hyattsville, Monroe Township, Miami County, Ohio. The records also indicate that Shotwell's childhood home was about three miles west of Hyattsville, a suburb of Tippecanoe, and that Tippecanoe was about six miles from Troy, Ohio. The records further establish that in 1861, Shotwell's sister, Emeline, married a man from Troy, who died about 1865. The records show that Shotwell's father sold his land in Monroe Township in 1863 and, in 1870, was living in Brooklyn, New York, with his wife and three daughters, one of whom was Emeline.

Charles A. Shotwell also stated in his November 22, 1924, letter to Reid that his boyhood friend told him:

---

[106] Second Amended State's Memorandum of Law, Exhibit 119 (C. A. Shotwell to Charles I. Reid, November 22, 1924).

of several of his experiences as a Soldier, one was of his being in Sherman's Army when it marched "Thru Georgia" to the sea. He told me of the Army going into the City of Raleigh, North Carolina (The Capital of the State), and said that the City had been set on fire by the retreating Confederates before the Union Army entered the City. The Union Army, he said, thoroughly sacked that City. . . .[107]

The following documented historical facts establish the accuracy and truthfulness of this portion of Shotwell's account. Sherman's 100,000-man army occupied Raleigh from April 13 to mid-May 1865. Approximately 20,000 members of the army were soldiers from Ohio. The 1860 United States federal census establishes that in that year 778 males, ages 12 to 45, were living in Monroe Township, Miami County, Ohio, which included the towns of Tippecanoe and Troy. All of these males would have been eligible for military service during the Civil War. An analysis of the muster rolls for Ohio regiments, the compiled service records of individual Union soldiers maintained in the National Archives, and the Civil War Soldiers and Sailors System database establishes that at least 81 men from Miami County were in Ohio volunteer regiments that passed through or occupied Raleigh in April-May 1865 as part of Sherman's army. Before retreating from Raleigh on April 12, 1865, Confederate troops set fire to a railroad depot on Lane Street between Blount and Salisbury streets at approximately the current site of the Legislative Office Building. The fire was not widely reported contemporaneously, and, therefore, its occurrence likely would have been known only by persons who were in Raleigh at the time of the fire or shortly thereafter, or by scholars of military history.

Shotwell's letter to Reid also states that his boyhood friend

> was one of a Company of Soldiers, that went through the State House and helped themselves there, to whatever they pleased to take. They went into the Office of the Secretary of State and forcibly took what they thought was worth carrying away. On opening a vault there, they found several boxes locked, which they proceeded to open and from one of them he took the parchment which I now have in my possession. He told me how he had brought it with him as a Soldier out of the State, so it was contraband of War and lawfully his possession.[108]

Members of Sherman's army were notorious for taking Confederate government property for personal use or gain or as souvenirs. In April 1865, when Sherman's army arrived in and occupied Raleigh, the manuscript Bill of Rights was stored in the State Capitol. One of the places where the document likely was stored was the secretary of state's office located on the Capitol's first floor in the north wing. Most members of Sherman's army had unfettered access to the Capitol, including the unoccupied secretary of state's office. By secret resolution, the North Carolina General Assembly had authorized funding for the secretary of state to have constructed crates or

---

[107] Second Amended State's Memorandum of Law, Exhibit 119 (C. A. Shotwell to Charles I. Reid, November 22, 1924).

[108] Second Amended State's Memorandum of Law, Exhibit 119 (C. A. Shotwell to Charles I. Reid, November 22, 1924).

boxes to use for packaging and transporting out of Raleigh some of the state's archival papers. The secretary of state's office did not, however, contain a vault; the only vault in the Capitol was in the treasurer's office.

There is no historical evidence that Shotwell's account of the circumstances under which he came into possession of the Bill of Rights is untrue. Rather, the account Shotwell provided in his letter to Reid is consistent with the version he gave many years earlier to a newspaper reporter. As originally reported by the *Indianapolis News* on May 10, 1897, an original copy of the Bill of Rights was possessed by Charles A. Shotwell, who was quoted as stating:

> I was living at Troy, O[hio], at the close of the war, thirty-two years ago. I got it off a soldier in an Ohio regiment. I believe it cost me $5. He took it from the State House at Raleigh, N.C. when that place was pillaged by Sherman's army.[109]

In a conversation with the Indiana secretary of state, who was assisting the North Carolina secretary of state in attempting to recover the stolen Bill of Rights, Shotwell confirmed the accuracy of his statement as reported in the newspaper article.

There is one significant misstatement in Shotwell's November 22, 1924, letter to Reid. Shotwell says that his friend told him that the Bill of Rights "was contraband of War and lawfully his possession." The Union soldier who took the Bill of Rights from the State Capitol had no authority to do so and violated military law by taking the manuscript for personal gain. The military law in effect at the time also prohibited the soldier from taking or passing lawful title of the Bill of Rights. Title to public property lawfully seized by the Union army occupying Raleigh was vested in the United States.

General Order No. 100, *Instructions for the Government of Armies of the United States in the Field*, was promulgated by President Lincoln on April 24, 1863. The *Instructions*, which were applicable to all Union troops during the Civil War, read, in pertinent part:

> Art. 44. . . . [A]ll destruction of property not commanded by the authorized officer, all robbery, all pillage or sacking, even after taking a place by main force, . . . are prohibited *under the penalty of death.* . . .
>
> A soldier, officer or private, in the act of committing such violence, and disobeying a superior ordering him to abstain from it, *may be lawfully killed on the spot by such superior.*
>
> Art. 45. *All captures and booty belong, according to the modern law of war, primarily to the government of the captor.* . . .
>
> Art. 46. Neither officers nor soldiers are allowed to make use of their position or power in the hostile country for private gain, not even for commercial transactions otherwise legitimate. . . .
>
> Art. 47. Crimes punishable by all penal codes, such as arson, murder, maiming, assaults, highway robbery, theft, burglary, fraud, forgery, and rape, if committed by an American soldier in a hostile country against its inhabitants, are not only punishable as

---

[109] *Indianapolis News*, May 10, 1897.

at home, but in all cases in which death is not inflicted the severer . . . punishment shall be preferred (emphases added).[110]

W. Hays Parks, senior associate deputy general counsel, International Affairs Division, Office of General Counsel, U.S. Department of Defense, is an internationally recognized expert in the field of the law of war. Parks has indicated that, in his opinion, "If an archival paper of the State of North Carolina, including a manuscript Bill of Rights, was taken by a Union soldier from the State Capitol in April-May, 1865 for personal use or gain, such taking was unlawful and illegal under the law of war then in effect and, therefore, title to the manuscript remained in its original owner—the State of North Carolina." Parks also offered his opinion that, "Whether the seizure of the manuscript Bill of Rights was authorized or unauthorized under the law of war, under no circumstances could the individual soldier who seized such property have acquired title to the property or the right to transfer title of the manuscript to another."[111]

Dr. Joseph Glatthaar, a nationally recognized Civil War historian and an expert on Sherman's campaign through the Carolinas and the military law applicable to Union armies during this period, has indicated that "if the manuscript Bill of Rights . . . was taken by a Union soldier from the North Carolina Capitol in April-May, 1865 for personal use or gain, either with or without authority of the soldier's superior officers, such taking was a violation of General Order No. 100." Dr. Glatthaar concluded that "legal title to public property of North Carolina that was captured or seized during the Civil War, including public property left behind in the Capitol by retreating state officers, could not pass to an individual." It is also Dr. Glatthaar's opinion that if the manuscript Bill of Rights was taken from the State Capitol by an individual Union soldier or was found abandoned and taken by a Union soldier, it immediately became property of the United States pursuant to General Order No. 100.[112]

Anecdotal evidence exists that General Sherman strictly enforced General Order No. 100. The May 18, 1865, edition of Wisconsin's Janesville *Weekly Gazette* reported that a week before, Sherman's brother, United States senator John Sherman, had been presented with a fine horse captured in the South Carolina campaign. Senator Sherman required a pass from his brother before he could ship the horse north. The senator visited the general's headquarters to take care of what he considered the small matter of getting the pass:

> "It's a splendid horse, Cump," said the honorable Senator, "and if you'll just sign a permit I'll take him up in the boat with me."
>
> Cump replied, adjusting his shirt collar with both hands, "I'm very glad he's a good horse. We are very much in need of good horses in the army. I have some orderlies around headquarters that are d—d badly mounted."

110 *War of the Rebellion*, ser. 3, 3:148-164.
111 Second Amended State's Memorandum of Law, Exhibit 157 (affidavit of W. Hays Parks).
112 Second Amended State's Memorandum of Law, Exhibit 127 (affidavit of Joseph Glatthaar).

The grave and venerable Senator was taken aback by this, and again reminded the general that the horse had been presented to him, and was not government property.

"Can't let you have him, John. All the horses here belong to Uncle Sam. Individual titles ain't worth a cent," said Cump and so the Senator was cheated out of his present (emphasis added).[113]

General Sherman's refusal to let even his brother have a spoil of war illustrates the extent to which he followed General Order No. 100.

General Order No. 100 was supplemented by Special Order No. 88, issued in Raleigh on June 12, 1865, by General Schofield, via Lt. Col. J. A. Campbell. Special Order No. 88 directed the return of all archives and other property required by law to be kept in the custody of the North Carolina secretary of state. Special Order No. 88 states in pertinent part:

> Hon. C. R. Thomas having been appointed, by his Excellency the Governor of North Carolina, Secretary of State of the State of North Carolina all archives and other property required by law to be kept in his custody will be turned over to him. The Offices in the State Capitol heretofore occupied by the Secretary of State will be vacated for his use.[114]

Therefore, any archives removed from the custody of the secretary of state by United States troops, whether lawfully or unlawfully under General Order No. 100, were required to be returned to the State.

As an archival legislative record of the State, the Bill of Rights was not subject to capture under General Order No. 100. Even if it were subject to capture, it was ordered returned to the State under Special Order No. 88; therefore, no soldier could acquire individual title to the manuscript.

This evidence far exceeds the standard established in *West* for the State to prove that the Bill of Rights was stolen or otherwise improperly removed from a public archive.

AUTHORS' NOTE: On March 24, 2008, the Wake County Superior Court issued an order declaring

> North Carolina's Original Copy of the Bill of Rights, is a public record of the State of North Carolina, that the State never has abandoned, conveyed or in any way relinquished its ownership of the Bill of Rights, and that the State alone holds all legal and equitable right, title and interest in the Bill of Rights to the exclusion of all other persons.

[113] Janesville, Wisconsin, *Weekly Gazette*, May 18, 1865.

[114] Special Order No. 88, June 12, 1865, Governors' Papers, William W. Holden, G.P. 185, North Carolina State Archives; also transcribed in Governors' Letterbooks, William W. Holden, G.L.B. 51, p. 1, North Carolina State Archives.

FIRST AMENDMENT GUARANTEES OF FREEDOM OF ASSEMBLY AND OF THE RIGHT TO PETITION

By Julius L. Chambers

EDITOR'S NOTE: Noted attorney and civil rights advocate Julius LeVonne Chambers was born in Mount Gilead, North Carolina. He earned a B.A. in history from North Carolina College (now North Carolina Central University) and an M.A. in history from the University of Michigan. In 1962, he graduated at the top of his class at the University of North Carolina School of Law, where he was the first African American editor of the *North Carolina Law Review*. He received a Master of Law degree from Columbia University Law School in 1964. Chambers worked for the National Association for the Advancement of Colored People (NAACP) Legal Defense and Education Fund before he opened a private practice in Charlotte in 1964. He helped to form the first biracial law firm in the state in 1967. His firm argued many notable civil rights cases, including the Wilmington Ten, and several landmark Supreme Court cases that challenged discrimination in employment and school busing. In 1968, Chambers was appointed to a commission to study changes to the state constitution. He left private practice in 1984 to become director-counsel of the NAACP Legal Defense and Education Fund. In 1993, he became chancellor of his alma mater, North Carolina Central University, where he served until returning to his Charlotte law firm in 2001. Chambers has taught at the University of Virginia Law School, the University of Pennsylvania, Columbia University Law School, and the University of Michigan Law School. He has written articles for publication in *The State of Black America* (1990), *The Warren Court: A Retrospective* (1996), and *African Americans and the Living Constitution* (1996). He presented these remarks at the ImaginOn performing arts center in Charlotte on October 5, 2007.

I was asked to speak about our Constitution's First Amendment guarantees of freedom of assembly and of the right to petition our government for redress of grievances. While I am honored to join the Bar Association and the North Carolina Office of Archives and History in lifting up and celebrating our Constitution and the reclamation of our state's copy of the Bill of Rights, I am not sure that I bring you the same fervor or excitement that the Bar Association and the Office of Archives and History may have anticipated or desired in inviting me.

As I reflect on this occasion, I think of comments made by the actor Charlton Heston in 1997 when he celebrated the role of white men in the nation's founding, saying: "The Constitution was handed down to guide us by a bunch of those wise old dead white guys who invented this country." While I, too, appreciate the Founding Fathers' wisdom in framing the Constitution, and I believe that our constitutional rights to freedom of assembly and to petition our government for redress of grievances are implicit in ordered liberty, I also find myself agreeing with Justice Thurgood Marshall, who, during our country's bicentennial celebration of the Constitution, said that he could not accept that the document we reflect on today is frozen in time with its meaning "forever fixed at the Philadelphia Convention." Rather, he said, "The Constitution as originally adopted was fundamentally flawed with the built-in provision to

The *Liberty and Freedom* tour was well attended at each stop, drawing large crowds of North Carolinians who wished to view their copy of the Bill of Rights. Image courtesy of the State Archives, N.C. Office of Archives and History, Raleigh.

correct the wrongs in ways that would meet our citizens' needs as we evolve as a society." The Constitution was and was meant to be a living, evolving instrument that would allow for the emergence of "framers" with every new generation of citizens who seek or sought social change. I believe that without this evolution there would be no cause for celebration this evening. There would be no pride in exhibiting a piece of parchment that represented a concept of freedom that applied only to white males who owned property.

There would be very little reason to celebrate if the ratification of the original document had not been followed with amendments, wars, and major social movements that dramatically changed our country and constantly shaped our modern view of "constitutional rights." Indeed, the true significance of the Constitution and of the Bill of Rights lies in our citizens' drive to correct injustice and social wrongs, in the right to assemble and petition to provoke change, and finally, in the awesome responsibility that we have to continue to transform this document and give true power to contemporary "framers."

As Justice Marshall also pointed out in his celebration speech, the first three words of the Constitution demonstrate the evolving nature of this foundational document. The words, "We the People," meant something entirely different in 1776 than they do today. Clearly, this phrase did not welcome a majority of the American people into these newly defined rights. We should not forget the fact that, I, a black American, would have been defined as "property," the status of slaves that was affirmed in the *Dred Scott* decision by the United States Supreme Court in 1857.

In our celebration we cannot ignore the fact that, despite the fierce debate about slavery and the status of slaves, the Constitution's framers—even those in staunch opposition to slavery and everything that it represented—compromised and carefully crafted a document that took special care to avoid mention of this heinous institution. After debate between delegates supporting and opposing slavery, the framers at the Constitutional Convention compromised, affirming the status of property to "all other Persons," meaning slaves, and defining each one as only three-fifths of a person with no right to vote. I would have had the freedom only to assemble where I was ordered; the only petition that I reasonably could have made with any hope of redress of my grievances would have been to God. Individuals would suffer the grips of slavery for many years after the institution was abolished by the Thirteenth Amendment, and after U.S. citizenship was defined in the Fourteenth Amendment as being "All persons born or naturalized in the United States and subject to the jurisdiction thereof." We were made citizens of the United States but still not accorded the kind of equal rights that others enjoyed.

The Fourteenth Amendment did not include as citizens another significant segment of individuals born in the United States—Native Americans—who were not granted U.S. citizenship until 1924. The guarantees of the U.S. Constitution have stayed more or less beyond the reach of Native Americans, who, in a "Protest of the Cherokee Nation" sent to Congress in 1836, aptly stated their unfortunate plight in their native land: "Little did [the Cherokee] anticipate that when taught to think and feel as the American citizen, and to have with him a common

African Americans vote in the Democratic Party primary election in Columbia, South Carolina, in 1948, the first time they had been allowed to do so since 1876. Photograph by Alexander M. Rivera Jr., courtesy of North Carolina Central University, Durham, N.C.

interest, they were to be despoiled by their guardian, to become strangers and wanderers in the land of their fathers."

The Fifteenth Amendment to the Constitution gave African American men, in principle, the right to vote. However, this amendment did not mention gender, so voting rights became an issue for women, who had no right to vote and were not hired and promoted on the same basis as others. They, too, used the First Amendment rights of freedom of assembly and petition for redress of grievances to challenge the treatment that they were receiving. It was through their protests, marches, assembling together, and petitioning the government that the Nineteenth Amendment to the Constitution was ratified in 1920 and gave women the right to vote.

African Americans benefited from the Voting Rights Act of 1964, which was passed by Congress as a result of petitions to the government and the assembling of people who were the victims, particularly in the South, of laws that, though they did not mention race specifically, were racially discriminatory in regard to voting rights. My father tried numerous times to register to vote in Mt. Gilead, North Carolina, and was not allowed to vote on the basis of literacy tests that did not actually measure literacy but included a requirement to interpret any conceivable section of the Constitution; often white examiners were not able to interpret the sections that they required of blacks who were attempting to register to vote.

I imagine that most of us here today would agree that these circumstances do not fit the image of a "more perfect Union" that you and I would accept and often take for granted. But considering the magnitude of the progress we have made since the drafting and adoption of the Constitution, I can say that as a nation we probably have relied on the provisions of the right to assemble and the right to petition our government more effectively than on any other section of the Constitution. They have made it possible to extend the Constitution to many more citizens without war or a major constitutional crisis. Every American citizen has the equal right and ability to unite with others to pursue change in our nation's political and electoral processes and to petition the government to right their wrongs.

Looking back, I consider the historical progression of the very meaning of the "right to peaceably assemble." In outlining some key cases involving this provision, an Indiana University graduate student truly captured the essence of the framing and evolution of these constitutional provisions:

- In 1667, colony founder William Penn was arrested in London for giving a sermon to a group of Quakers in the street in front of his church. London officials had locked the hall and forbidden Penn "to preach in any building," so he began to preach his sermon in the streets. He was charged with unlawful, tumultuous assembly that disturbed the king's peace. The judge in the case tried to force the jury to return a verdict of guilty. Penn ultimately was discharged by order of the Lord President of Munster.

- In 1876, the Supreme Court ruled that the "right of the people peaceably to assemble for the purpose of petitioning Congress for a redress of grievances, or for anything else connected with the powers and duties of the national government, is an attribute of national citizenship, and as such, is under the protection of, and guaranteed by, the United States." The high court applied the liberty only to any federal government's encroachment.

- In 1937, the U.S. Supreme Court unanimously ruled that the right to peaceably assemble "for lawful discussion, however unpopular the sponsorship, cannot be made a crime." The decision applied the First Amendment right of peaceful assembly to the states through the due process clause of the Fourteenth Amendment.

- In 1939, the Court ruled that peaceful demonstrators may not be convicted for "disorderly conduct." This case also secured streets and sidewalks as public forums.

- In 1940, the Supreme Court held that orderly union picketing that informs the public of issues is protected by the constitutional freedoms of speech, of the press, and of the right to peaceable assembly, and cannot be prosecuted under state loitering and picketing laws.

- In 1963, the Court overturned the breach of peace convictions of 180 black students who had peacefully marched in South Carolina to the state capitol to protest racial discrimination. The police stopped the demonstration and arrested the students because they were afraid that the two to three hundred who had gathered to watch the demonstration might cause a riot. The Court held the state law unconstitutionally over-broad because it penalized the exercise of free speech, peaceable assembly, and the right of petition for a redress of grievances. A disorderly crowd, or the fear of one, cannot be used to stop a peaceful demonstration or cancel the right of peaceable assembly.

In recent times, particularly during the civil rights movement, freedom of assembly was used frequently in order to defend Dr. Martin Luther King Jr. and the other peaceful demonstrators who protested Jim Crow laws and practices. Freedom of assembly and petition have been linked in legal cases in order to force the government to expand the meaning of the Constitution and to open up opportunities for women, minorities, and others.

We had the problems with blacks in education—they were not exposed to the same education as others. We had a long fight with efforts of blacks to obtain equal educational opportunities. We eventually obtained several decisions that required equal treatment of blacks and whites in education, and one can go down the list with several things we have been able to accomplish in this connection, including the elimination of discrimination in employment, in voting, and in housing, as well as in other areas.

We can look at how these two freedoms—the freedom of assembly and the freedom to petition our government—have worked together, for example, in order to expand opportunities in the Montgomery bus boycott in 1955-1956. The governmental powers in Montgomery, Alabama, had decided that they would end the bus boycott by, among other methods, arresting blacks who were carpooling in private automobiles to avoid riding the buses. They arrested and charged them with operating taxis without a license. They did this because they could not arrest them for assembling together in a vehicle. They couldn't legally pass a law that barred two or more blacks from sitting in a car. They had to say you are not running a taxicab or you do not have the proper license—there was always a pretext—they did not succeed in doing exactly what they wanted to do even though they tried really diligently. The fact that they used those tactics is in some way indicative of how enshrined the rights of assembly and petition are in our system; the authorities tried to use underhanded means to accomplish their illegal purposes in Montgomery for more than a year, but ultimately those efforts failed.

In my own work, as I was suing school systems, businesses, and others on behalf of clients who were being discriminated against, my home and my car were bombed, and my office was burned and destroyed. To the extent that people disagreed with me, and to the extent that people wanted to prevent me from doing what I was trying to do, they had to do those kinds of illegal, underhanded, anonymous acts because they could not go to the City of Charlotte and say, "This Chambers guy is causing trouble; you need to throw him in jail."

As recently as two weeks ago, the right to assemble protected the public protests and marches in Jena, Louisiana. Local people were on television, saying the same things that governmental officials had said in Mississippi during the summer of 1964 when many people converged to help with getting blacks and the poor registered to vote: "We can handle our own problems; the people coming in here are the ones making trouble." But they could not stop the assembling of people from all over the country. I was proud to see on television the busload of students from my alma mater, North Carolina Central University, who traveled to Jena to make their voices heard in protesting what they perceived as an injustice. The grievances as protected by the Constitution were different from those of forty-some years ago, but the need for justice and individual respect has not changed over the years.

We had problems in the beginning when African Americans were not even recognized as human beings or as citizens, but we have advanced over these years. I think that what we have seen in terms of a living Constitution should give encouragement to all of us that we can continue to evolve principles to protect all people. We have reached the point today, largely through the exercise of the First Amendment right to petition the government for grievances and freedom to assemble, where we do provide, potentially, equal opportunities for minorities and women and the poor—well, not quite the poor yet—but we are making some progress. We still have major problems with discrimination against the poor. We enact pilot programs and all kinds of legislation but still cannot bring ourselves to really address the kinds of difficulties that poor people bring to the table. We have a Supreme Court that still refuses to find that discrimination against people because they are poor violates the Constitution as much as discrimination based on race and color and gender.

More importantly to me, much of the progress that we have made over the past thirty years in opening up opportunities for minorities and women is now being seriously challenged by the Supreme Court and Congress. Many of the school districts desegregated after years of litigation and stress are now resegregating with the approval of the Court. In two recent decisions, the Court has made it more difficult to preserve or achieve desegregation, racial and ethnic, in the schools. However, with what we have seen in the Constitution and in the hopes and encouragement it gives all of us in the belief and confirmation that working together, and with all Americans, we can build a better country that will accommodate all of our differences and aspirations.

There are a number of accomplishments we should be able to use. First, we know that we can use the Constitution to effect change, even on preserving the desegregation we have obtained. We also know we can continue to use the Constitution to evolve principles to protect the poor. I still believe that the poor constitute a suspect class and that their claims for an education, or healthcare, or housing, or employment, can be shown to involve fundamental rights.

We celebrate the Constitution today, particularly the two provisions we have discussed, in order to help all of us appreciate that our Constitution is a living document that can evolve to insure protection for all Americans. We have seen how it has evolved over the years.

We also celebrate the Constitution today to highlight that there is still much work to be done. There are social and legal inequities that must be and will be addressed because our citizens will not sit idly by as children, families, and communities face injustice and inequality. Individuals and groups will continue to unite and petition their government for changes, such as strengthening democratic participation by protecting the right to vote; improving public education by achieving diverse, high performing schools for all children; and empowering neglected minority and lower income communities by outreach, mobilization, and civic engagement.

I have been involved in major civil rights activities for more than forty years, and in just a matter of a decade, I have watched many hard-fought gains slip away. Schools are resegregating, particularly in the South; minority communities are struggling to retain rights to their land and to increase the value of their assets; and redistricting proposals and other changes to election methods are going forward at the expense of minority representation. Courts are denying review of civil rights cases on appeal, and claims of discrimination go unrepresented as lawyers shy away from unpopular cases that are difficult and expensive to push forward. There has to be a counterforce against efforts by so many institutional pressures to bury civil rights activity. If we do not keep pushing, we will certainly lose all the ground for which so many fought and died.

In light of the uncertainties that the recent Supreme Court voluntary integration decision creates for school boards' use of race-conscious measures, it is critical that we continue to mobilize communities and petition our school boards, commissioners, and courts to ensure that we foster equal diverse/equal educational opportunities for all students—demanding adequacy and equality in schools and combating school resegregation.

Voting rights have continued to be challenged, most recently in Indiana, which passed a law giving that state the strictest voter identification requirements in the nation. Under the bill, most voters would have to show a photo ID issued by the federal or state government, such as a military ID or a driver's license. The freedom of petition was invoked by the Indiana Civil Liberties Union because of concerns that the bill is unconstitutional and unfair to those who don't have a government-issued photo ID, such as a driver's license, and may not be able to get one. Opponents contend that the law will burden voters, particularly the elderly and the poor, who possess driver's licenses or passports in fewer numbers. Courts in several other states are considering the constitutionality of similar laws.

Cases like these simply demonstrate that there is work to be done and the importance of how the freedoms of assembly and petition may change the minds of society. I don't discount the advancements that we have made as a country. We have seen significant changes in the last four to five decades as our nation has grown. However, I also cannot avoid seeing that there is still a struggle. We continue to fight to counteract the results of the flawed government that was largely framed by the Constitution, which was, as Justice Thurgood Marshall observed, "a product of its times, and embodied a compromise which, under other circumstances, would not have been made." The battle may not be as outwardly visible as it was in the 1960s and 1970s, but trust me when I say that every day people throughout this country face challenges to their rights to share in this nation's opportunities for healthy, whole, and free lives.

We have a responsibility to view the history of our Constitution soberly and contemplatively so that we don't lose the true significance of what it represents. It represents opportunity to progress and grow as a nation and to ensure that those who lack opportunity and resources are acknowledged and represented.

Today I would like for us to take Justice Marshall's words to heart, and as we celebrate the Bill of Rights as a foundational document, remember that we must also "commemorate the suffering, struggle, and sacrifice that has triumphed over much of what was wrong with the original document and observe [this occasion] with hopes not realized and promises not fulfilled." Yes, let us take this opportunity to celebrate a document that has evolved with our nation as the American people and our needs have changed. Just take special care to remember that inasmuch as the original framers contributed to the Bill of Rights, we are here to celebrate today every advocate, attorney, protester, and concerned citizen who has joined with others to petition and assemble in the name of social justice and since then has accepted the charge to push forward as a contemporary "framer" of this same document.

On April 18, 1957, Dr. Martin Luther King Jr. spoke at a youth march for integrated schools, saying:

> Whatever career you may choose for yourself—doctor, lawyer, teacher—let me propose an avocation to be pursued along with it. Become a dedicated fighter for civil rights. Make it a central part of your life. It will make you a better doctor, a better lawyer, a better teacher. It will enrich your spirit as nothing else possibly can. It will give you that rare sense of nobility that can only spring from love and selflessly helping your fellow man. Make a career of humanity. Commit yourself to the noble struggle for human rights. You will make a greater person of yourself, a greater nation of your country, and a finer world to live in.

Though he was speaking to young people, his words speak also to a greater value that embraces the very nature of our nation's modern interpretation of our right to peaceably assemble and petition the government for the redress of grievances. Each member of our nation has been granted the opportunity, right, and responsibility to stand up alone or with the support of others, and seek justice and change. We have the power to write the next evolutional level of the Constitution through our actions and our willingness to commit ourselves to the justice and equal opportunity for all people. In the words of Justice Ruth Bader Ginsburg, "Even if the culture of the framers held them back from fully perceiving that universal ideal [of equal dignity of all persons] . . . we can best celebrate that legacy by continuing to strive to form 'a more perfect Union' for ourselves and the generations to come." For the young people in the audience today, and others who speak and understand their current language, I will quote from Oprah Winfrey, who, after a lawsuit in which she was found not liable in exercising cherished First Amendment rights, said, "The First Amendment rocks!"

"ADDITIONAL GUARDS FOR LIBERTY": THE RIGHTS TO TRIAL BY JURY AND DUE PROCESS OF LAW

By Willis P. Whichard

EDITOR'S NOTE: Willis Padgett Whichard is "the only person in the history of North Carolina who has served in both houses of the state legislature and on both of the state's appellate courts." Born in Durham in 1940, Judge Whichard earned degrees from the University of North Carolina at Chapel Hill (A.B. and J.D.) and the University of Virginia (LL.M., S.J.D.). He served as law clerk to Justice William H. Bobbitt of the North Carolina Supreme Court in 1965-1966 and then joined the Durham law firm of Powe, Porter, Alphin, and Whichard. He was elected to the North Carolina House of Representatives in 1970 and to the state senate four years later. In 1980, he was appointed (and later elected) to the North Carolina Court of Appeals. He served as an associate justice of the North Carolina Supreme Court from 1986 to 1998. Judge Whichard was named dean of the School of Law at Campbell University in July 1999; he retired in 2006. He is the author of *Justice James Iredell* (2000), a biography of the first North Carolinian to serve on the U.S. Supreme Court. Judge Whichard currently works with the law firm of Moore and Van Allen. He gave the following presentation at the University of North Carolina at Asheville on November 9, 2007.

The time was late July and early August 1788. The place was the Presbyterian church in the small inland North Carolina town of Hillsborough. The occasion was the first of two conventions to determine the momentous question of whether North Carolina should ratify the proposed federal Constitution.

Willie Jones of Halifax, probably the state's leading Anti-Federalist, wanted to simplify and hasten the whole process. Once preliminaries were disposed of, Jones moved that the question upon the Constitution be put immediately. The subject, he said, had been debated at length throughout the country. The delegates had had ample opportunity to consider it; and they were, he thought, quite ready to vote.

James Iredell of Edenton, the Federalists' leader, was horrified. The question before them was one "of great consideration." "A Constitution like this," he said, "ought not to be adopted or rejected in a moment." He shuddered at the thought of going home and telling his constituents that he had voted on so fateful a question "without any previous consideration."

On this issue Iredell prevailed, as the convention, by a wide margin, voted to discuss the Constitution clause by clause. When the ultimate question was put, however, the Federalist leader would not be so fortunate. Both the weather and the debates were hot, but one objection to the proffered document overrode all others: there was no bill of rights.

Samuel Spencer, Iredell's former colleague in the state's judiciary, had voiced the common concern. "Our rights are not guarded," he said:

> There is no declaration of rights to secure to every member of the society those inalienable rights which ought not to be given up to any government. Such a bill of rights would be a check upon men in power. . . . There ought to be a bill of rights, in

order that those in power may not step over the boundary between the powers of government and the rights of the people, which they may do when there is nothing to prevent them.

Later in the convention, William Lenoir echoed Spencer's sentiments. "It is natural for men to aspire to power," he said. "[I]t is the nature of mankind to be tyrannical; therefore it is necessary for us to secure our rights and liberties."

Lenoir correctly noted that amendments were desired by other states. North Carolina was not alone in its concerns. They were held on a sufficiently widespread basis that a five-foot, four-inch, one-hundred-pound Virginian—a shy intellectual with a quiet voice—undertook to do something about them. James Madison already had a substantial investment in the proposed governing document. While at the Philadelphia convention, he had wanted future generations of Americans to know why the Framers had written the Constitution the way they did; as a consequence, without missing a day, he took notes of almost everything said that was important and recorded all votes. Later he would say that his note-taking duties that summer almost killed him. Having already made an outlay of that magnitude, he was not at all willing to lose the venture now.

Interestingly, this required something of a volte-face for Madison. For several years he had written disparagingly about a bill of rights. In *Federalist 38* he had dismissed the need for a list of rights on the grounds that the Anti-Federalists could not agree on what protections they wanted, noting that the absence of a bill of rights in the confederation presumably proved that the nation could manage without one. In *Federalist 46* he implied that a bill of rights was unnecessary because the states could protect citizens from an oppressive federal government. Finally, in *Federalist 48* he argued that a bill of rights would do little good because states had already proven that they were able to infringe personal liberty despite explicit protection in state constitutions or a declaration of rights.

Over time, under the gentle but firm persuasion of Thomas Jefferson and others, Madison softened his opposition. Once he perceived that the promise of a bill of rights was essential to bring about the new government, supporting it became easy for him.

Securing a position from which to accomplish it, however, would be anything but easy. Patrick Henry was the leading Anti-Federalist in Madison's state of Virginia. By artfully drawing the boundaries of the state's congressional districts, Henry and his allies hoped to prevent Madison's election to the House of Representatives. They also asked James Monroe—war hero, widely respected political figure, and, like Madison, a future president—to run against Madison.

The Anti-Federalists almost succeeded. The shy and reserved Madison was forced to campaign so actively that he incurred a frostbitten nose, which continued to bear the mark. He pledged that, if elected, he would work for safeguards for "all those essential rights, which have been thought in danger." Articles, letters, personal appearances, and the efforts of friends spread the word about Madison's commitment to a bill of rights.

All the efforts were necessary, as Madison prevailed on a bitter cold election day by a margin of only 336 votes. He had made a promise to the citizens of his district and state that, if elected, he would work diligently to support amendments to protect individual liberty, and he kept it.

On May 4, 1789, Madison rose from his seat in the House of Representatives to announce that on May 25 he would introduce a discussion of amendments to the Constitution. He managed to insert into George Washington's inaugural address a section that he hoped would launch a successful debate on amendments. The opposition would be vocal and formidable; but largely by dint of the little man's perseverance, the Congress approved, the required number of states ratified, a second constitutional convention—which could have been disastrous—was averted, and the country got its Bill of Rights.

Article III, Section Two of the Constitution mandated jury trials in criminal cases. Madison undoubtedly knew that the absence of a provision preserving that right in civil trials was a major concern of those opposed to the Constitution. His fellow Virginian, George Mason, had refused to sign the proposed Constitution in Philadelphia and was opposing ratification by Virginia. Mason's primary objection was the lack of a bill of rights, and he especially regretted the absence of language protecting trial by jury in civil cases. Thomas Jefferson, to whom Madison was especially close, wanted to see a right to trial by jury in all cases. In the Virginia ratifying convention, John Dawson had criticized the absence of a bill of rights, mentioning in particular the failure of the Constitution to include trial by jury in civil cases. Madison's collaborator on the *Federalist Papers*, Alexander Hamilton, had written in number 83 that the principal objection to the Constitution in his state of New York, as well as in several others, was "that relative to the want of a constitutional provision for the protection of trial by jury in civil cases."

State constitutions sometimes covered the federal omissions, but the constitutions of five of the states did not protect the right to trial by jury in civil cases. Madison thus expressly included it in his January 1789 list of essential rights that he thought the Constitution should be amended to protect.

It is a myth that the civil jury system is a uniquely American institution. Its origins have been traced to ancient Egypt circa 2000 B.C. Our English ancestors were guaranteed the right in the Magna Carta, signed by King John at Runnymede in 1215.

Trial by jury, if we use the term in a large sense, neglecting some technical details, was introduced by the ordinances of Henry II as part of the usual machinery of civil justice. From this point forward, other proofs are being pushed into the background. The abolition of the trial by ordeal in 1215 left a gap. The truth of a matter could no longer be tested, as it once was, by heat or water, and the duel was out of the question. So the verdict of a jury emerges as the only possible mode of proof; it offered a decision based upon facts rather than divine miracles, as in the instance of trial by water, fire, or other ordeal. Litigants became dependent, not on divine interference in human affairs, but on the verdict of their peers.

The jurors must be free and lawful, impartial and disinterested, neither the enemies nor the too close friends of either litigant. Their verdict becomes not just the decision of twelve men; it is the verdict of a neighborhood, a community, a state, a country. Gradually, other forms of resolving disputes are abandoned.

Unanimity comes to be required. Arbitral and communal principles triumph. Parties to litigation put themselves to a certain test. That test is the voice of the country. Just as a corporation can have but one will, so a country can have but one voice.

The whole system of trial by jury in its earliest form implies representation—a person is tried by the country, by the neighborhood. The voice of the jurors is the verdict of the country, *veredictum patriae*. A litigant puts himself on his neighborhood, for good or for ill.

Sir William Blackstone summed up well when he wrote:

> Here, therefore, a competent number of sensible and upright jurymen, chosen by lot from among those of the middle rank, will be found the best investigators of truth, and the surest guardians of public justice. For the most powerful individuals in the state will be cautious of committing any flagrant violation of another's right, when he knows that the fact of his oppression may be examined and decided by twelve indifferent men, not appointed until the hour of trial; and that, when once the fact is ascertained, the law must of course redress it. This, therefore, preserves in the hands of the people that share which they ought to have in the administration of general justice, and prevents the encroachments of the more powerful and wealthy citizens.

The American Founders were quite familiar with the practice. Thomas Jefferson's initial draft of the Declaration of Independence contained, in its litany of abuses for which it skewered the king, the phrase, "for depriving us of the benefits of trial by jury." The convention, more concerned with complete accuracy than Jefferson had been, inserted the words, "in many cases," thereby conceding that the deprivation, while it had occurred, had not been universal.

Six of the states—Massachusetts, New Hampshire, North Carolina, Pennsylvania, Vermont, and Virginia—provided for trial by jury in civil cases in their declarations or bills of rights. Virginia, for example, provided "[t]hat in controversies respecting property, and in suits between man and man, the ancient trial by jury is preferable to any other, and ought to be held sacred." North Carolina's provision read essentially as it does today: "In all controversies at law respecting property, the ancient mode of trial by jury is one of the best securities of the rights of the people, and shall remain sacred and inviolable."

This provision was dispositive in one of the most significant cases in the early American republic. *Bayard v. Singleton* is best known as one of a handful of state cases that established the principle of judicial review of the constitutionality of legislative acts well before John Marshall ensconced it into the fabric of the American experiment in the federal case of *Marbury v. Madison*. It is of at least equal importance, however, as an early and controversial, but ringing, affirmation of the right to jury trial in civil cases.

The case is rooted in the prosecution of Loyalists in the wake of the American Revolution. The plaintiff had acquired considerable property from her father, a Loyalist who had fled the state of North Carolina for exile in New York. The defendant had purchased the property at a sale provided for in the state's 1785 Confiscation Act. The act provided that titleholders under lawfully conducted confiscation sales did not have to respond to suits by those with conflicting claims. The courts were to dismiss such actions upon the mere presentation of motions or affidavits accompanied by deeds from confiscation commissioners showing *prima facie* title in the defendants. Seeking unmistakable clarity, the General Assembly provided that the statute applied notwithstanding "any law, usage or custom to the contrary."

The statute, however, butted heads with the state constitutional right to trial by jury. It was clear to the court, as expressed by Justice Samuel Ashe, "that no act [the legislators] could pass could by any means repeal or alter the Constitution, because if they could do this, they would at the same instant of time destroy their own existence as a Legislature, and dissolve the Government thereby established." The court thus simultaneously preserved both the supremacy of constitutions over statutes in the hierarchy of legal authority and a state-level right to trial by jury in civil cases.

The fact that some states were preserving and enforcing a right to trial by jury in civil cases did not satisfy the Anti-Federalists. During the ratification process, Richard Henry Lee of Virginia was among the first of several Anti-Federalists to declare misleadingly that the Constitution, if ratified, would abolish trial by jury in civil cases. That was one of the most frequently trumpeted Anti-Federalist charges. Lee invoked Sir Edward Coke, Sir Matthew Hale, Sir John Holt, Blackstone, and almost every other legal or political writer to prove that trial by jury in civil cases was an essential right necessary to maintain freedom and to keep courts from becoming arbitrary. Patrick Henry alleged that the Constitution jeopardized trial by jury. The influential minority report of the Anti-Federalists in Pennsylvania declared that trial by jury in civil cases ought not to be abolished. An essay by an anonymous writer in a Philadelphia newspaper grieved over the death of "that sacred bulwark of liberty," trial by jury in civil cases. "Centinel," a prolific Philadelphia newspaper essayist, predicted that the federal courts would "supersede the state courts" because the Constitution failed to provide for civil jury trials. A writer to a Boston newspaper insinuated that an inquisition would be the result of abolishing trial by jury in civil cases.

The foregoing simply illustrates the routine in Anti-Federalist rhetoric and publications. It, of course, did not stand unanswered. Alexander Hamilton offered the fullest and best repudiation in *Federalist 83*, in which he discoursed on the differences in state practices and on the power of Congress to establish courts and therefore trial by jury.

In his *Commentaries on the Constitution*, Justice Joseph Story quotes the Seventh Amendment: "In suits at common law, where the value in controversy shall exceed twenty dollars, the right of trial by jury shall be preserved, and no fact tried by a jury shall be otherwise re-examined in any court of the United States than according to the rules of the common law." He then notes that this amendment "struck down the objection" and "secured the right of a trial by jury, in civil cases, in the fullest latitude of the common law." The right, he said, is an "inestimable privilege" and "essential to political and civil liberty."

Karl Llewellyn, perhaps the foremost legal scholar and educator of his day, has noted that "a jury of the vicinage" can set law and government "at naught" and find so-called "facts" in the teeth of the truth, all in the interest of the prevailing emotions and prejudices of the vicinage. Llewellyn was positing the concept of jury nullification. An old story best illustrates it.

A defendant named Tom was on trial for killing a deer out of season. He testified that he knew that it was not deer season and was aware of the illegality of his action, but that his children were hungry, and he had no other source of food for them. The jury acquitted, and the judge later asked the foreman how it could have done so in the face of an uncontroverted admission of guilt. "Well, Your Honor," came the reply, "you instructed that the credibility of the evidence was for us to determine, and we just didn't believe old Tom when he said he shot that deer."

Most, if not all of us, would agree with the jury in Tom's case. Clearly, the jury can be a means to overcome the harshness of the positive law and avert results that we would consider unjust. When the positive law arrays itself against the clear, stable, considered desires of a majority of a vicinage, juries may simply decline to enforce it. Jury independence asserts itself when the law exceeds the limits of social consensus; it goes into hibernation when the law has been reformed; and it re-emerges when legislative ambition again overtakes its legitimate bounds.

We find perhaps the foremost example of this in the failed American experiment with the prohibition of alcoholic beverages. The attempt criminalized a social custom that was deeply ingrained in, and widely accepted by, American culture. The basic American right to be let alone, except when one's conduct infringes upon the rights of others, was also implicated and threatened. The laws, as a consequence, were routinely rejected by independent American juries. In some areas of the country, as many as 60 percent of alcohol-related prosecutions ended in acquittals. Twenty-six percent of the National Prohibition Act cases filed in federal courts nationwide ended in acquittals. Where juries did convict, they often returned compromise verdicts that resulted in reduced punishments for the accused.

Prohibition has been described as a "crime category in which the jury was totally at war with the law." "Since men began making laws," Clarence Darrow observed, "the favorite form of repeal is by non-observance." The experiment with prohibition is clearly an instance in which the verdicts of independent juries contributed to a change in the law.

While our sympathies might be with the juries in those cases, jury nullification also has an ignoble history. During the civil rights movement, many southern juries refused to convict avowed racists for heinous crimes. The most odious charge against independent juries is that they cannot be trusted to do justice when a white person is on trial for crimes or civil wrongs against a black victim. This history is most commonly invoked against jury independence. It is vividly and movingly depicted in one of the twentieth century's greatest novels, Harper Lee's *To Kill a Mockingbird*, in which a black man named Tom is convicted by an all-white Alabama jury of a crime he clearly could not have committed.

Other great works of literature also provide social commentary on the institution of the jury. In Charles Dickens's first novel, *The Pickwick Papers*, Mr. Pickwick becomes a boarder with a Mrs. Bardell, and the arrangement becomes the basis of her suit against him for breach of promise to marry. Pickwick is discussing the matter with his friends when Mr. Snodgrass wonders what the foreman of the jury had for breakfast. "'Ah!' said Mr. Perker, 'I hope he's got a good one.' 'Why so?' inquired Mr. Pickwick. 'Highly important, very important, my dear sir,' replied Perker. 'A good, contented well-breakfasted juryman is a capital thing to get hold of. Discontented or hungry jurymen, my dear sir, always find for the plaintiff.' 'Bless my heart,' said Mr. Pickwick, looking very blank, 'what do they do that for?' 'Why, I don't know,' replied the little man coolly, 'saves time, I suppose.'" He goes on to say that the approach of dinnertime in the late afternoon may well also produce a rather hasty verdict for the plaintiff.

Later in the episode Dickens spoofs both the pomposity of counsel and the egoism of jurors. Witness this brief excerpt:

> Sergeant Buzfuz began by saying, that never, in the whole course of his professional experience—never, from the very first moment of his applying himself to the study and practice of law—had he approached a case with feelings of such deep emotion, or with such a heavy sense of responsibility imposed upon him—a responsibility, he would say, which he could never have supported, were he not buoyed up and sustained by a conviction so strong that it amounted to positive certainty that the cause of truth and justice, or, in other words, the cause of his much-injured and most oppressed client, must prevail with the high-minded and intelligent dozen of men whom he now saw in that box before him.

> Counsel usually began in this way, because it puts the jury on the very best terms with themselves, and makes them think what sharp fellows they must be. A visible effect was produced immediately; several jurymen beginning to take voluminous notes with the utmost eagerness.

Still later, Sergeant Buzfuz concludes his jury argument as follows:

> "But Pickwick, gentlemen, Pickwick, the ruthless destroyer of this domestic oasis in the desert of Goswell Street—Pickwick, who comes before you to-day with his heartless Tomata sauce and warming-pans—Pickwick still rears his head with unblushing effrontery, and gazes without a sigh on the ruin he has made. Damages, gentlemen—heavy damages—is the only punishment with which you can visit him; the only recompense you can award to my client. And for those damages she now appeals to an enlightened, a high-minded, a right-feeling, a conscientious, a dispassionate, a sympathizing, a contemplative jury of her civilized countrymen." With this beautiful peroration, Mr. Sergeant Buzfuz sat down, and Mr. Justice Stareleigh woke up.

Then from Lewis Carroll's *Alice's Adventures in Wonderland* we get Alice's dream of the trial of the Knave of Hearts, in which the twelve jurors are writing busily on their slates before the trial begins. "To what purpose? Alice inquires. 'They're putting down their names,' the Gryphon whispered in reply, 'for fear they should forget them before the end of the trial.' When Alice accidentally knocks all of the jurymen out of the box, she puts the lizard back in head downwards and is puzzled when ordered to put all the jurymen back in their proper places. 'I should think it would be *quite* as much use in the trial one way up as the other,' she protests."

Finally in this regard, there is the transformative experience of Mr. Henry Bosengate of the London Stock Exchange in John Galsworthy's short story, "The Juryman." Mr. Bosengate had such a sense of self-importance that "[t]o be summoned to sit on a jury at the local assizes, and not even the grand jury at that . . . was in the nature of an outrage." By the time he completed the trial of a soldier charged with attempted suicide because he could not endure the separation from his wife, however, he was a changed man who insisted on mercy. He had learned that "Life's a wonderful thing, a thing one can't live all by oneself; a thing one shares with everybody, so that when another suffers, one suffers too." "It's come to me," he says, "that what one *has* doesn't matter a bit—it's what one does, and how one sympathizes with other people." Watching "that poor little rat of a soldier in his trap," he said, was the first time that he had felt "the spirit of Christ." "We've got to be kind, and help one another," he concluded, "and not expect too much and not think too much."

As we conclude our consideration of the right to trial by jury, we should mention briefly the American Board of Trial Advocates (ABOTA). This organization was formed in 1958 based on the perception that the right to trial by jury "was coming under heavy fire." Its principal purpose is to "[e]ncourage respect for the law, the courts, and the right to trial by jury." It defines its membership as those "who know that the jury's Constitutionally mandated role is as the protector of the rights of person and property." It advocates the continuing viability, almost eight hundred years later, of the provision of the Magna Carta that "no freeman shall be seized, imprisoned, or dispossessed . . . excepting by the judgment of his peers."

The system that ABOTA exists to protect constitutes a democratic institution within the judicial branch in which the public regularly participates and makes decisions. It is a bulwark against the tyranny of power. No significant deprivation of property can be accomplished in a civil suit without participation of a jury, unless that right is waived. The system incorporates important community values into the deliberative process and ensures that the legal system does not stray too far from the judgment of the larger community. Jury verdicts, in the aggregate, generally accord with community norms, and this in turn enhances the legitimacy and viability of the outcome.

Quotations from two well-known Englishmen provide a summation. In 1956 Winston Churchill said: "The jury system has come to stand for all we mean by English justice. The scrutiny of twelve honest jurors provides Defendant and Plaintiff alike a safeguard from arbitrary perversion of the law." The writer G. K. Chesterton has said:

> Our civilization has decided, and very justly decided, that determining the guilt or innocence of men is a thing too important to be trusted to trained men. If it wishes for light upon that awful matter, it asks men who know no more law than I know but who can feel the things that I felt in the jury box. When it wants a library catalogued, or the solar system discovered, or any trifle of that kind, it uses up its specialists. But when it wishes anything done that is really serious, it collects twelve of the ordinary men standing about. The same thing was done, if I remember right, by the Founder of Christianity.

The Great Charter, as Blackstone called the Magna Carta, not only provided that "no free man shall be taken or imprisoned or disseised or outlawed or exiled, or in any way ruined . . . except by the lawful judgment of his peers." The very

Supreme Court justice Oliver Wendell Holmes adopted his own basic litmus test for defining due process of law. Image courtesy of the Library of Congress, Prints and Photographs Division, Washington, D.C.

next clause required that such be done "by the law of the land." As far back as the reign of Edward III, the phrases "law of the land" and "due process of law" have been equivalent in legal parlance. Like the right to trial by jury, this concept found its way into the American Bill of Rights. Amendment Five provides that "[n]o person shall . . . be deprived of life, liberty, or property without due process of law." The post-Civil War Fourteenth Amendment applied the concept to the states.

The right to trial by jury is quite tangible. The right to due process of law is not. It is much more easily defined by negative than by positive expression. A story is illustrative.

When Harlan Fiske Stone was chief justice of the U.S. Supreme Court, he came to Justice Oliver Wendell Holmes's office one day with the plaintive question, "What is due process?" Justice Holmes responded by saying politely, "Young man, why don't you sit down?" (Holmes was in his early nineties; Stone, in his early sixties.) When the younger man had seated himself, Holmes continued by saying, "Now, why don't you ask me what *isn't* due process?" Stone complied, and Holmes responded, "It isn't due process when it makes me vomit."

Consideration of due process would be relatively simple if it involved nothing more than the application of Justice Holmes's regurgitation-production test. Even then, however, some of us rest more easily in both the stomach and the conscience than do others. Even apart from idiosyncratic digestive variances, the subject is far more complex.

Sir Edward Coke set forth in his *Second Institutes*, published in 1642, a series of common law rights that protected the freeman's life and liberty. Due process of law was among them. Earlier, in *Dr. Bonham's Case*, Coke had placed a gloss upon the phrase, stating that "when an Act of Parliament is against common right or reason, or repugnant, or impossible to be performed, the common law will control it and adjudge such Act to be void." Several of the American colonies anticipated or followed Coke and provided for the right in their fundamental documents. An "Act for the liberties of the people" approved by the Maryland General Assembly in 1639 assured Maryland freemen (not slaves) that they would "not be imprisoned nor disseissed or dispossessed of their freehold goods or chattels or be outlawed, exiled or otherwise destroyed, fore judged or punished" without due process of law. In 1641 the Massachusetts Bay Colony promulgated a document styled "the Body of Liberties." Various of its provisions prohibited authorities from depriving a citizen of life, liberty, or property without due process of law. The West New Jersey proprietors agreed that no freeholder or inhabitant could be deprived of life, liberty, or property "without a due trial." New York's 1683 "Charter of Libertyes and Priviledges" provided that such could not be done except "by the Law of this province." In North Carolina's original constitution, such was to be by the law of the land, and in South Carolina's, with the observance of due process of law. The ordinance of 1787 relating to the Northwest Territory likewise contained a law-of-the-land provision.

So what is the "law of the land" or "due process of law"? Probably the most oft-quoted definition is that given by Daniel Webster in the *Dartmouth College* case. "By the law of the land," Webster said, "is most clearly intended the general law; a law which hears before it condemns; which proceeds upon inquiry, and renders judgment only after trial. The meaning is that every citizen shall hold his life, liberty, property, and immunities under the protection of the general rules which govern society. Everything which may pass under the form of an enactment is not therefore to be considered the law of the land."

The design is to exclude arbitrary power from every branch of the government. All persons have a right to require that their controversies shall be judged by the same rules that are applied in the controversies of their neighbors. The community as a whole is entitled, at all times, to demand the protection of the ancient principles that shield private rights against arbitrary interference, even though such interference may be under a rule impartial in its operation. It is not the partial nature of the rule so much as its arbitrary and unusual character that condemns it as unknown to the law of the land.

A New York case states it thusly: "Due process of law undoubtedly means in the due course of legal proceedings, according to those rules and forums which have been established for the protection of private rights." The U.S. Supreme Court has said: "[A]fter volumes spoken and written with a view to their exposition, the good sense of mankind has at length settled down to this, —that [the words of the Magna Carta] were intended to secure the individual from the arbitrary exercise of the powers of government, unrestrained by the established principles of private rights and distributive justice." Finally in this regard, Thomas Cooley's nineteenth-century *Treatise on the Constitutional Limitations* says that "[d]ue process of law in each particular case means such an exertion of the powers of government as the settled maxims of law permit, and under such safeguards for the protection of individual rights as those maxims prescribed for the class of cases to which the one in question belongs."

Notwithstanding the elegance of these attempts at definition, it is little wonder that for centuries jurists and lawyers have struggled to give the words content and meaning in individual cases; that their results have not always met with universal acceptance; or that consensus, when achieved, has often been fleeting. The abiding struggle to achieve the ideals that the words represent is simply a part of the constantly evolving Anglo-American common law tradition from which we should expect no permanent escape.

We can say with confidence, however, that fair procedures always have been, and are today, at the heart of the concept. One procedural essential is an accessible, impartial, and effective decision maker. It was recognized early that the law could not make a man a judge in his own case. In *Dr. Bonham's Case*, Coke attempted to give content to the law's restraint on power and to impart substance to due process; he thought the procedural horror of making a man a judge in his own case the example on which all could agree. The common law, he thought, would certainly void a statute so contrary to "common sense and reason." Madison, perhaps influenced by Coke, spoke to this in number 10 of the *Federalist Papers*. "No man," he wrote, "is allowed to be a judge in his own cause, because his interest would certainly bias his judgment, and, not improbably, corrupt his integrity." As recently as my tenure on the North Carolina Supreme Court, that court said emphatically that "[d]ue process requires a neutral decision-maker."

Yet, for a century and a half, a number of American states allowed something very similar to judging one's own case. Magistrates or justices of the peace, the lowest rung on the judicial ladder, were paid from the fines they levied. It was not until 1928 that the U.S. Supreme Court declared the longstanding practice unconstitutional. Citing *Dr. Bonham's Case*, the Court relied on Coke's reasoning, with Chief Justice William Howard Taft stating that for a case to be decided by a judge with "a direct, substantial, pecuniary interest" in its outcome is a deprivation of due process.

Making a man a judge in his own case was, then, the paradigm of a violation of natural justice and a prime example of a deprivation of due process. Justice Samuel Chase mentioned this in the 1798 case of *Calder v. Bull*, but then proceeded to give another example: "a law that takes property from A and gives it to B." "It is against all reason and justice . . . for a people to entrust a Legislature with such powers," wrote Chase, "and therefore, it cannot be presumed that they have done it." A half century later, Justice Samuel Miller was more explicit. A statute that took property from A and vested it in B, he said, "would, if effectual, deprive A of his property without due process of law."

Chase placed in the same category "[a] law that punished a citizen for an innocent action"; that is, "for an act, which, when done, was in violation of no existing law." We now refer to these as *ex post facto* laws, with which the common law of England was replete. Jeremy Bentham has cynically observed, "The common law is made by the judges on the same principles as a man makes laws for his dog—he waits till the dog has done something he does not like and then punishes him for it."

In appealing to "reason and justice," Chase was sounding a natural law theme, which did not go unchallenged. Justice James Iredell in reply denied that judges could be guided by so uncertain a rule. "The ideas of natural justice are regulated by no fixed standard," wrote Iredell. "The ablest and purest minds have differed upon the subject." Scholars generally consider Iredell's the prevalent view for nearly a century, but Chase's ultimately triumphant, though styled as "substantive due process." One writes, descriptively and aptly:

> In practice, . . . some of the [U.S. Supreme] Court's more recent decisions under such rubrics as "substantive due process" raise the question whether it is paying lip service to Iredell for the sake of appearances while effectively following Chase—a course of action that arguably compounds usurpation with deception.

This substantive due process jurisprudence provided the germ of a response when, in the late nineteenth century, regulatory legislation threatened vested economic interests and individual entrepreneurship. If taking from A and giving to B was a violation of due process, merely taking from A could be as well, thus bringing a wider range of legislation within the concept's prohibitory ambit. The paradigm due process case of taking from A and giving to B became a powerful weapon against regulatory legislation. In a notorious 1911 decision, *Ives v. South Buffalo Railway Co.*, New York's highest court used both the "law of the land" phrase and the "A to B" paradigm in invalidating that state's pioneering Workmen's Compensation Act. "When our Constitutions were adopted," the court said, "it was the law of the land that no man who was without fault or negligence could be held liable in damages for injuries sustained by another." To change that principle by imposing liability on one who had omitted no legal duty and committed no wrong was, the court said, "taking the property of A and giving it to B, and that cannot be done under our Constitution."

Application of substantive due process to regulatory legislation reached its most notorious fruition in the federal courts. The U.S. Supreme Court, for example, invalidated a federal statute setting minimum wages for women in the District of Columbia because it took from A and gave to B. The legislation, the Court said, amounted to "a compulsory extortion from the employer for the support of a partially indigent person for whose condition there rests upon him no particular responsibility, and therefore, in effect, arbitrarily shifts to his shoulders a burden which, if it belongs to anybody, belongs to society as a whole." The broader implication was that taking away the freedom to contract was just as bad, and therefore just as forbidden, as taking something from A and giving it to B.

One case in this line gave its name to an entire era in the history of due process from the 1890s to the 1930s. In *Lochner v. New York*, the U.S. Supreme Court invalidated a New York statute limiting bakers to sixty hours of labor a week or ten hours a day. The Court held the act not reasonably related to any of the social ends for which government power might validly be exercised and therefore a violation of the due process clause. Due process now had a substantive rather than merely a procedural meaning, and by the 1930s economic substantive due process and other legal doctrines restricting economic regulation had become a political issue of the greatest magnitude.

In the middle of that decade, however, a hotel chambermaid named Elsie Parrish asked an obscure lawyer in Wenatchee, Washington, to sue her employer for back pay based upon the employer's violation of that state's minimum wage law. She could not possibly have realized that she was launching a constitutional revolution. Indeed, in light of four decades of Supreme Court jurisprudence, and particularly the Court's decision holding a federal minimum wage act unconstitutional as violating the liberty of contract guaranteed by the Constitution, her case must have seemed hopeless. It would have been expected that any law that transgressed the due process clause of the Fifth Amendment, which applied only to the federal government, would, if enacted by a state, be held to violate the due process clause of the Fourteenth Amendment, which applied to the states.

The economic substantive due process doctrine had its critics, however, including Chief Justice Charles Evans Hughes and Justice Harlan Fiske Stone. Stone, in particular, had accused his colleagues in the majority of indulging their "own personal economic predilections." "The Fourteenth Amendment," he had written, "has no more embedded in the Constitution our preference for some particular set of economic beliefs than it has adopted, in the name of liberty, the system of theology which we may happen to approve."

With President Franklin Roosevelt's court-packing plan lurking in the background, Justice Owen Roberts altered his usual position and voted to sustain the Washington minimum wage law. His vote changed the majority. Justice George Sutherland still thought that the due process clause embraced freedom of contract, and he said so in a vigorous dissent. As an eminent historian has written, though, he surely knew that the decision in Elsie Parrish's case had "[blown] taps for the nineteenth-century world." Congressman Maury Maverick called it "the Greatest Constitutional Somersault in History." "For," he said, "Owen Roberts, one single human being, had amended the Constitution by nodding his head instead of shaking it. The lives of millions were changed by this nod." The Court had ceased the practice of striking significant national and state socioeconomic legislation on grounds that it violated economic substantive due process.

Liberty subsequently came to be defined in terms other than economic. The due process clause evolved into the primary source of unenumerated, non-economic individual rights, especially in cases involving human reproduction. In 1965, in *Griswold v. Connecticut*, the Supreme Court invalidated a state statute prohibiting artificial birth control because it invaded "zones of privacy" recognized by various amendments in the Bill of Rights and applied to the states by the Fourteenth Amendment. The due process clause of the Fourteenth Amendment was the vehicle through which specific parts of the Bill of Rights, otherwise applicable only to the federal government, were applied to the states. The Fifth Amendment's due process clause was not invoked. *Griswold* opened a new era of substantive due process, one concerned with rights other than economic.

The most familiar manifestation of the change is the 1973 abortion decision in *Roe v. Wade*. The statute at issue was held to violate a woman's right to privacy, now simply described as an aspect of liberty. It was, the Court held, violative of the due process clause of the Fourteenth Amendment. The due process clause thus is now itself the source of the prohibition rather than merely the conduit through which various provisions of the Bill of Rights are applied to the states. Concurring in *Roe*, Justice Potter Stewart illuminated the new understanding of the earlier birth control case. "The *Griswold* decision," he wrote, "can be rationally understood only as a holding that the Connecticut statute substantively invaded the 'liberty' that is protected by the Due Process Clause of the Fourteenth Amendment." Subsequent justices and commentators have accepted Justice Stewart's re-characterization of *Griswold* as a substantive due process case.

Today, almost eight centuries after armed English barons forced King John to swear not "to go or send against any free man except *per leggem terrae*" (by the law of the land), due process still forbids, and probably always will, unfair procedures. It means, at the least, as the North Carolina Supreme Court stated in 1994, " 'notice and an opportunity to be heard and to defend in an orderly proceeding adapted to the nature of the case before a competent and impartial tribunal having jurisdiction of the cause.' " It incorporates the principles of adversarial fairness, said our court, requiring a " 'balance of forces between the accused and his accuser.' " It dictates that there be no punishment of a defendant prior to an adjudication of guilt.

Like our Supreme Court, the U.S. Supreme Court has catalogued certain basic requirements of procedural due process: adequate notice, an opportunity to be heard, the right to present evidence, confrontation of opposing witnesses, the right to cross examine those witnesses, disclosure of adverse evidence, the right to an attorney if desired, a decision based solely on the evidence produced at the hearing, a statement of the reasons for the decision, and—as noted—an impartial decision maker.

Substantive due process, as the foregoing treatment illustrates, is a much more variable concept. It can mean unfettered economic liberty in one period of history and unrestricted reproductive freedom in another. Formerly the watchdog of the free market, it can metamorphose into the guardian of privacy in intimate personal relations. It is a matter on which, as Justice Iredell reminded Justice Chase so long ago, "the ablest and purest minds have differed." It is altogether reasonable to predict that while procedural due process will remain reasonably well defined and clearly understood, substantive due process will continue to be both mutable and the subject of differences among the ablest and purest minds.

SUGGESTED READINGS

Books

Amar, Akhil Reed. *America's Constitution: A Biography*. New York: Random House, 2005.

Amicus Curiae, ed. *Law in Action: An Anthology of the Law in Literature*. New York: Crown Publishers, 1947.

Boorstin, Daniel J. *The Mysterious Science of the Law*. Boston: Beacon Press, 1941.

Cohen, William, Jonathan D. Varat, and Vikram Amar. *Constitutional Law: Cases and Materials*. 12th ed. New York: Foundation Press, 2005.

Conley, Patrick T. and John P. Kaminski. *The Bill of Rights and the States: The Colonial and Revolutionary Origins of American Liberties*. Madison, Wis.: Madison House, 1992.

Conrad, Clay S. *Jury Nullification: The Evolution of a Doctrine*. Durham, N.C.: Carolina Academic Press, 1998.

Cooley, Thomas M. *A Treatise on the Constitutional Limitations Which Rest Upon the Legislative Power of the States of the American Union*. Boston: Little, Brown and Company, 1883.

Elliot, Jonathan. *The Debates in the Several State Conventions on the Adoption of the Federal Constitution as Recommended by the General Convention at Philadelphia in 1787*. 5 vols. Philadelphia: J. B. Lippincott Company, 1907.

Hale, Matthew, Sir. *The History of the Common Law of England*. Chicago: University of Chicago Press, 1971.

Hand, Learned. *The Bill of Rights*. Cambridge, Mass.: Harvard University Press, 1958.

Holdsworth, William. *Some Makers of English Law*. Cambridge: Cambridge University Press, 1966.

Labunski, Richard. *James Madison and the Struggle for the Bill of Rights*. Oxford: Oxford University Press, 2006.

Leuchtenburg, William E. *The Supreme Court Reborn: The Constitutional Revolution in the Age of Roosevelt*. New York and Oxford: Oxford University Press, 1995.

Levy, Leonard W. *Origins of the Bill of Rights*. New Haven: Yale University Press, 1999.

London, Ephraim, ed. *The World of Law: The Law in Literature*. Vol. I. New York: Simon and Schuster, 1960.

Maier, Pauline. *American Scripture: Making the Declaration of Independence*. New York: Alfred A. Knopf, 1997.

Maitland, F. W. *The Constitutional History of England*. Cambridge: Cambridge University Press, 1963.

Orth, John V. *Due Process of Law: A Brief History*. Lawrence: University Press of Kansas, 2003.

Pollock, Frederick, Sir, *Jurisprudence and Legal Essays*. London: Macmillan and Company, Ltd., 1961.

Pollock, Frederick, Sir, and Frederic William Maitland. *The History of English Law*. 2 vols. Cambridge: Cambridge University Press, 1968.

Pound, Roscoe. *The Development of Constitutional Guarantees of Liberty*. New Haven: Yale University Press, 1957.

Rutland, Robert Allen. *The Birth of the Bill of Rights, 1776-1791*. Chapel Hill: University of North Carolina Press, 1955.

Taswell-Langmead, Thomas Pitt. *English Constitutional History from the Teutonic Conquest to the Present Time*. Boston: Houghton Mifflin, 1919.

Whichard, Willis P. *Justice James Iredell*. Durham, N.C.: Carolina Academic Press, 2000.

Articles

Chandler, George E. "Memories of Patriots from Texas to Washington." *Voir Dire* (winter 2003): 14-18.

Geer, David. "North Carolina: Bringing Us the Seventh Amendment and the Bill of Rights . . . Twice." *Voir Dire* (summer 2003): 5-7.

Monserratte, Patrick D. " 'Why Are You Here?' " *Voir Dire* (winter 2002): 4-7.

Nockleby, John T. "What's a Jury Good For?" *Voir Dire* (summer 2005): 6-11.

INDEX

Constitution, 44; requests President Washington to transmit proposed Bill of Rights to states, 36, 44

First Federal Congress Project: staff of, examines Bill of Rights, 39-40, 58; staff of, examines photographs of Bill of Rights, 39, 57, 67; staff of, identifies Bill of Rights as North Carolina's copy, 39-41, 60, 67

First New Haven Capital Corporation, 56, 57

Forbes, Malcolm, 37

Fourteenth Amendment: defines citizenship, 89; due process clause of, 91, 104, 108, 109; removes freedom of press issues to federal courts, 9

Fourteenth Army Corps, 48-49

Fox, George, 16, 17

Freear, Richard, 69

Freedom of assembly: applied by Supreme Court to permit union picketing, 91; extends Constitution to more citizens, 91; guaranteed by First Amendment, 87; included in Declaration of Rights (1774), 4; protects protesters during civil rights movement, 92; used by women to challenge gender discrimination, 90

Freedom of religion: can be prohibited by states, 1; in colonial America, 15-19; in North Carolina, 17, 19-20; threats to, in Western Europe and England, 15-17; in Virginia Bill of Rights and constitution of 1776, 19

Freedom of speech: applied by Supreme Court to protect union picketing, 91; fundamentally different from freedom of the press, 9-10; history of, 26; prior to American Revolution, 4; threats to, in twentieth century, 8

Freedom of the press: amorphousness of, 5-6; applied by Supreme Court to protect union picketing, 91; in colonial America, 4-5; defined by Supreme Court in twentieth century, 9; effects of information technological advances on, 10; in England, 3-4, 9; fundamentally different from freedom of speech, 9-10; guaranteed in first state constitutions, 5; included in Declaration of Rights (1774), 4; restricted by states during

Revolutionary War, 5; threatened by Andrew Jackson and Abraham Lincoln, 8; threatened by Sedition Act of 1798, 6-7; threats to, in North Carolina, 8-9; threats to, in twentieth century, 8-9

French Revolution, 6, 26

Freneau, Philip, 6

Fries, John, 7

G

Gales, Joseph, 6

Gallatin, Albert, 7

Galsworthy, John, 102-103

Gazette of the United States, 6

General Order No. 100, 84-86

George III, 19, 30

Georgia, 31, 37, 38, 46

Gerry, Elbridge, 29-30, 32

Gilbert, Sir Humphrey, 2

Ginsburg, Ruth Bader, 95

Glatthaar, Joseph, 85

Glorious Revolution of 1689, 3

Government House, 49

Grayson, William, 34, 36, 37-38

Green, James, 74

Griswold v. Connecticut, 108-109

H

Hale, Sir Matthew, 100

Hamilton, Alexander, 6, 98, 100

Hamilton, Andrew, 4

Hamilton, J. G. de Roulhac, 54-55

Hamilton, John, 78

Harmelin, Stephen, 60, 61

Hawkins, Benjamin, 78

Helper, Hinton Rowan, 8

Henderson, Pleasant, 69-70

Henry II, 98

Henry VIII, 15

Henry, Patrick, 34, 36, 97, 100

Heston, Charlton, 87

Hill v. Colorado, 26

Hillsborough, N.C.: as site of first constitutional convention in state, 5, 21-22, 25, 44, 96

Historical Society of Pennsylvania, 36

Hobart, Harrison C., 48

Holmes, Oliver Wendell, 104

Holt, Sir John, 100

Hooper, William, 64

ratifies Bill of Rights, 37; ratifies
    Constitution, 31-32
Southern Illinois University, 51
Special Order No. 88, 52, 86
Spencer, Samuel, 96-97
St. Mary's Hospital, 49
St. Thomas Episcopal Church, 18
Stamp Act of 1765, 3, 4-5
Stanly, Edward, 13
State Capitol: duties and activities of
    Union soldiers in, 49-51, 83; office of
    secretary of state in, turned over to
    carpetbagger successor, 52, 86; public
    records in, stolen by Union soldiers,
    14, 50-53, 81; public records stored in,
    48, 51, 74-75, 80-81; U.S. Army Signal
    Corps station established at, 50
State House, 47-48, 80-81
State Library of North Carolina, 47
State of North Carolina: awarded
    ownership of Bill of Rights, 86; claims
    ownership of Bill of Rights, 61;
    interest in Bill of Rights conveyed to,
    by Wayne E. Pratt, 61-63; refuses to
    pay for return of Bill of Rights, 14,
    55-56. *See also* North Carolina
State of North Carolina v. B. C. West Jr.: as
    precedent for ruling in Bill of Rights
    case, 62, 63-67, 72, 75-76, 79-81
Stevenson, George, Jr.: defines court of
    record, 72-73; defines duty of House
    of Commons to preserve public
    records, 73, 80; identifies Bill of Rights
    as North Carolina's copy, 61, 67-70, 80
Stewart, Potter, 109
Stokes, Montfort, 69
Stone, Harlan Fiske, 104, 108
Story, Joseph, 100
Substantive due process, 107-109. *See
    also* Due process of law
Sullivan, John, 36-37
Sutherland, George, 108

T

Taft, William Howard, 106
Tenth Amendment, 14, 32, 34
Test Act (1704), 17
Thirteenth Amendment, 2, 89
Thomas, Charles R., 52, 86
Thomas, William Holland, 52
Thompson, Cyrus, 53-54

Tillou, Peter H., 59, 60
To Kill a Mockingbird, 101
Torsella, Joseph, 60, 61
Townsend Acts, 4-5
Treatise on the Constitutional Limitations,
    105-106
Trial by jury: Anti-Federalists want
    guaranteed in civil cases by
    Constitution, 100; guaranteed in civil
    cases by some states, 98, 99; included
    in Declaration of Rights (1774), 4; in
    literature, 101-103; mandated by
    Constitution in criminal cases, 98;
    origins of, 98-99; predates Magna
    Carta, 2
Tryon, William, 17
Tucker, St. George, 38
Tucker, Thomas Tudor, 38
Turner, Josiah, 52
Turner Broadcasting v. the FCC, 26
Twentieth Army Corps, 49
Twenty-seventh Amendment, 44
Twenty-third Army Corps, 49

U

U.S. Army Signal Corps, 50
U.S. Army Signal Corps Photographic
    Unit, 54
U.S. Attorney's Office, 60
U.S. Congress: challenges legal
    advancements made by women and
    minorities, 93; passes Voting Rights
    Act of 1964, 90; rejects religious test
    for public office, 23
U.S. Constitution: certified copy of, in
    N.C. State Archives, 77; as living,
    evolving document, 87, 89, 93, 95;
    mandates trial by jury in criminal
    cases, 98; North Carolina refuses to
    ratify, because lacking Bill of Rights,
    96; ratification of, 31-32, 44; ratifica-
    tion of, by North Carolina, 5, 22, 37,
    46; ratification of, as victory for
    Federalists, 2
U.S. Court of Appeals for the Fourth
    Circuit, 62-63
U.S. District Court for the Eastern
    District of North Carolina, 60, 61, 62,
    63
U.S. Supreme Court: affirms property
    status of slaves, 89; applies freedoms

of speech, press, and assembly to protect union picketing, 91; applies right of peaceable assembly to states, 91; catalogues basic requirements of procedural due process, 109; defines freedom of the press in twentieth century, 9; invalidates Connecticut law prohibiting birth control, 108; invalidates New York statute limiting hours of work, 107; invalidates statute setting minimum wage for women in District of Columbia, 107; recent decisions by, affect freedom of speech, 26-27; recent decisions by, challenge legal advancements made by women and minorities, 93-94; refuses to find discrimination against the poor unconstitutional, 93; rules magistrates accepting fines they levied unconstitutional, 106; rules that rights of freedom of assembly and petition for redress of grievances are protected by federal government, 91; upholds minimum wage law, 108

Union Square, 49

V

Vance, Zebulon Baird, 48, 52

Veit, Helen, 40, 58

Virginia: applies to Congress for second constitutional convention, 34; appoints Anti-Federalists to U.S. Senate, 34; disestablishment of Anglican Church in, 20; has original copy of Bill of Rights, 38; ratifies Bill of Rights, 37-38; ratifies Constitution, 32

Virginia Charter of 1606, 2

Virginia Declaration of Rights (1776), 5, 19, 99

Virginia Gazette and Public Advertiser, 38

Virginia Statute of Religious Freedom (1786), 20

Voting Rights Act of 1964, 90

W

Wake County Superior Court, 43, 86

Walker, David, 8-9

Washington, George: alarmed by weakness of national government under Articles of Confederation, 21; certified copy of Cession Act sent to, 79; informs Congress that North Carolina has ratified Constitution, 46; location of letters from, transmitting copies of Bill of Rights, 36-37; mentions Bill of Rights in inaugural address, 98; persuaded by James Madison to support Bill of Rights, 34; presents to Congress enrolled copy of North Carolina statute ratifying Constitution, 47; transmits copy of proposed Bill of Rights to North Carolina governor, 14, 41, 46; transmits original copies of proposed Bill of Rights to states, 1, 36-37, 44, 46

Wayne Pratt, Inc.: claims ownership of Bill of Rights, 61; conveys interest in Bill of Rights to State of North Carolina, 61-63; has cardboard backing removed from Bill of Rights, 58; makes deposit for purchase of Bill of Rights, 56; offers to sell Bill of Rights to National Constitution Center, 59-60; purchases Bill of Rights, 59; retains lawyer to help buy and sell Bill of Rights, 56. *See also* Pratt, Wayne E.

Webster, Daniel, 105

West, B. C., Jr., 64

West New Jersey, 105

Westchester Gazette, 52-53

Wheeler, Joseph, 48

Wheelock, Samuel B., 51

White, John, 15

Williams, Roger, 17-18

Williamson, Hugh, 4

Winfrey, Oprah, 95

Worth, Daniel, 8-9

Worth, Jonathan, 52

Z

Zenger, John Peter, 4